Anger in Children
Causes, Characteristics and Considerations

Anger in Children
Causes, Characteristics and Considerations

Editor

Dr. H. L. Kaila

MD Publications Pvt Ltd
New Delhi

For information:

MD Publications Pvt Ltd
'MD House', 11, Darya Ganj
New Delhi - 110 002
Phone : +91-11-41563325 (Customer Service)
+91-11-41562846 (Editorial)
E-mail (orders): contact@mdppl.com
Website: www.mdppl.com

ISBN: 978-81-7533-150-1

Published and Printed by Mrs. Rajni Gupta on behalf of **MD Publications Pvt Ltd** at Times Press, New Delhi.

Contents

PREFACE

Schools, parents, teachers, policy planners, psychologists and educationists all over the world have been concerned in the management of anger in children for their healthier growth and development. Questions such as what are the determinants of anger in growing-up children and how does anger impact children mentally, socially and behaviorally are still unanswered. Towards this inquiry, several scholars have attempted to provide perspectives and perceptions on anger in children. Issues that have been dealt in this book are: children coping within a hostile environment; helping young children to manage with anger; self-identity styles, self-assertiveness and self-efficacy among adolescents; alternative model of emergence of mental health problems in children; gender differences on emotional intelligence, coping strategies and anxiety; burnout and anger in teachers and parents; impact of ICDS on development of children; early childhood stimulation in changing socio-cultural scenario; socio-cultural correlates of behavior problems in children; and changing social realties in teaching profession.

Dr. H. L. Kaila

Editor

Acknowledgement

We are indeed grateful to the following persons and institutions for their special contributions in the preparation of this manuscript:

Prof. Usha Ram
Dr B.J. Prashantham
Prof. Usha Nayar
Dr. K. B. Kushal
Dr. Vijayam Ravi
Ms Rekha Sahani
Dr. Sharmila Banwat
Dr. M. Puandhare
Mrs. Anita Sanu
Prof. V.V. Khole
Prof. C. Rybek
Dr. Harish Shetty
Dr. M. Deuskar
Dr. S. Jaya
Ms. Natasha D'Cruz
Dr. Swaroop Rawal
Counselors Association of India
Dayanand Institute of Education Manamgment & Research
Christian Counseling Centre
S.N.D.T. Womens' University
Singhania School Thane
D.A.V. Schools Panvel, Thane, Airoli, Nerul

And all the contributors, authors, teachers, students, counselors, principals, and the participants of the national conference on anger and development of children.

Dr. H. L. Kaila

ACKNOWLEDGMENT

[illegible]

1

ANGER AND DEVELOPMENT OF CHILDREN

Dr. Vijayam Ravi

He was an ordinary student in his teens. The bodily transitions in him into adulthood made him uncomfortable. The girl students teased him. He was growing more and more restless at the sarcastic remarks that he faced from fellow students and the girls. He wanted to retaliate. At a suitable occasion, he filled the water bottle of the girl whom he hated most, with his urine. The girl unknowingly drank the same. When she knew what had happened, it was too much for her and the damage was beyond repair. The anger and frustration of the boy knew no bounds and after that he was calm! Why did he do it? Could he have avoided it? How? What about the girl? Are the school and parents responsible for it? School Counselor was taken into confidence. A very in-depth enquiry revealed the issues of lack of support at home, school and community. A well thought structured program was designed for the boy which made him realize the mistake he committed. The mother was asked to keep good food habits for him reducing on the intake of non-vegetarian and junk food. This changed food habit calmed him down. The girl student also was counseled and it did take some time for her to get over it. Her parents were extremely cooperative. Two young lives were reformed with a proper intervention from adults.

Anger, Food habits, Interventions, Home, School, Community

There had been many interesting cases in my career as Principal for over two decades. These cases display the agony that children go through for no fault of theirs and how the interventions helped them come over the crisis.

Few cases of anger among children that I encountered:

1) This little boy was ten years old, fairly average in studies, coming from a noble family, who cares for education. However, the mother was very demanding and wanted the son to excel in studies always, without allowing him any free time to play with other children in his neighborhood. One fine day, the boy refuses to come to the school. The parents coaxed him to the school and brought him to the class. The teacher intervened to find out the problem, the counselor offered help but the boy was so scared that he would run away from the classrooms. He had somehow become, physically very aggressive. The boy was taken for treatment with a psychiatrist. The treatment continued with heavy doses of medicines and the boy was almost sleeping all the time. This demanded a medical leave for this boy. This was granted and the school extended support by giving him the lessons and assignments. Yet, he was uncomfortable and scared of something unknown. A very soft approach to him made me realize that he was scared of something which he was not able to explain. He started imagining some unknown voices urging him to jump from the building terrace or hang from the ceiling fan or hit the people whomever he sees. The parents were doing all that they could-mantra, tantra etc along with medicines! He was very confused about why he was behaving like this and hence I referred him to a doctor friend who handled it beautifully well. All the medicines which were given to him earlier were stopped. First of all the parents

were counseled, both by the doctor and the school. I suggested that the child can come to school, whenever he feels like attending, and he can play if he doesn't want to go to class. But, however he has to certainly come to my room and say "hello" to me every morning. He readily agreed. Today, he is a very cheerful child attending school regularly, doing his studies very well, and even, meets me once in a while.

Here we see anger or frustration, being expressed as fear.

2) This 12 years old boy was from the beginning very aggressive. He was not good at studies and didn't fare well academically. The teachers had tried their level best to bring him back to studies but he chose to violence. He indulged in hitting others, bullying the juniors in the school bus, spoiling their food, throwing their lunch boxes, using abusive language which is unheard of even from an adult, and abusing teachers. He was very unclean, drowsy all the time and not at all interested in studies. The counselor had intervened and I had also interfered when the teachers approached me. The parents were called for a discussion but the mother never turned up. The father wouldn't understand what we were saying, because according to him, his son was always right. We referred him to a psychiatrist but, the father never budged. As the school didn't believe in corporal punishment, the teachers were trying to persuade him through counseling. A quiet enquiry about his background brought to light, very startling facts. The boy was the son of a police officer who used to beat his son and wife at home, using abusive language. The son had been witnessing this scene almost daily. When this fact was known to me, the teachers were given some guidelines to treat this boy in a slightly different way. I would not say that it was a very successful attempt because the boy refused to budge. Finally, he left the school himself.

Here we see abusive language and violence as an after-effect of practices that are followed at home.

3) He was in the twelfth standard. His parents were living separately because of a marital discord. The father had an affair with his own sister, whom his wife could not accept and she became mentally ill. The son was living with the mother. The mother always doubted him. Any phone call, coming to the boy was scrutinized because she felt that her son was also leaving her. The mother also was suffering from some mental disorders for which she was undergoing a treatment herself. The boy who was a top ranker in his old school proved to be an academic failure in the 11th and 12th std. Almost, everyday he came to school with empty stomach, did not eat anything because his mother never gave him anything. After the school hours, he was playing basketball alone, even during late evenings. I noticed him, the teachers noticed him, counseling started and all the above said facts came to light. Many times the Vice Principal arranged to get him food from the canteen because we realized his hunger had made him anemic. Most of the time, he was sleeping in the class. The counselor took a great care about him. The parents were called but they refused to cooperate. During the public examination of 12th std, he sat in the examination hall and started blabbering about unrelated events and fainted. We all knew the importance of this one year in his life and hence I walked into the exam hall and gave him something to drink, called the doctor and in a tough voice I said, he cannot play up with his life and that he has to write the examination or else he will not meet me anymore. I have known earlier that this boy had tremendous amount of respect for me. I decided to capitalize on that. His father was called immediately and the vice principal intervened. From the next day onwards, the father was present with him till the examination time in school and made sure that he attends the examinations. He scraped through with a first class, but one day he came to my residence and cried his heart out and said that he doesn't want to see his parents

anymore and enquired with me whether I can help him to get him out of this country. I had only one answer to him, that running away is escapism and one should learn to put up with differences and disagreements with others. However, I advised him to apply to some foreign universities and finally he got into one and is doing well there. Once in a while, he gets in touch with me through e-mail to let me know that he is doing well.

Here we see withdrawal and self-denial as an example of lack of parental support.

Why such cases in Schools? What is wrong with our systems?

We hear many cases where children end their life, where teachers punish the children brutally, where children kill their parents!

- Why do we get angry?
- How do we act when we get angry?
- How do we evaluate the action?

These are the prominent questions that may provide answers while we discuss about development of children. Anger is very often used in the negative sense because of the way it is displayed. Sometimes it is a required emotion that can bring about positive changes also in the society. When one loses the nervous balance or control or poise, we come to know that he is angry. He can then become ugly and disastrous. When some external or internal humiliation occur, anger is aroused in a person and the outlet is vigorous. To relieve the anger some people indulge in physical violence or destructive activity.

Why do we get angry?

There may be hundreds of reasons for a person to get angry. As far as children are concerned, anger is a challenge to their parents, teachers and even the society. The reasons can be external stimuli like humiliation, fear, and lack of sleep, fatigue or the company of adults who are always angry at nothing. Temper tantrums are seen right from childhood and this is purely to gain attention. Physical causes also can prove to be the reasons for someone to get angry-like poor eye sight, bad food, hunger, dental cavities, stomach problems and not very good diet habits. Psychological reasons like humiliation, a sense of frustration or deprivation all can arouse anger in a child. In a fast moving world of today where every individual is busy with his/her priorities, there is no one to take care of the children with their **food habits** in many families. As a result, the children resort to junk food and food that has a lot of fat content. This results in an obese structure in children. It is proved beyond doubt that obese children are comparatively lethargic and tend to lose their cool easily. The Great text on psychological treatises, The Bhagavad Gita, talks about three Gunas or habits called Satwik, Rajasik and Tamasik which arise out of eating different types of food. Fresh vegetables and less spicy, warm fresh food belong to Satwik variety, excessively spicy, and over cooked and food that is old is Rajasik and spoilt food and food that is stored in the refrigerators and fatty cold food is Tamasik. The Tamasik food induces intoxication and aggressiveness in people due to the biological transitions in the organic matter and the Rajasik food induces temper tantrums in them. The Satwik food is the most ideal food for bringing up children. This excessive fatty food kindles their emotions at a wrong signal and they tend to react. Fresh vegetables have become a rarity in the diet for children.

According to Lewis and Michelson, (1983), there are three components for **anger.**

1. Emotional state of anger- that a person acknowledges that he is angry. This is very important. Asking children to do something when they really do not want to do it, physical assault like punishments, rejection etc is the different emotional states of anger.
2. Expression of anger- how does he express the anger- sometimes through crying, sulking, aggressive, revenge,

withdrawal etc.

3. Understanding of Anger - which means interpreting and evaluating the emotion called Anger.

Usually bottled up feelings come out as anger which is almost like explosive dynamite. Oxford Dictionary defines anger as **"Extreme displeasure".** It is considered as a negative feeling which is usually associated with punishment - both in the case of adults and children. However, I consider anger as a derived emotion from fear, lack of self esteem, respect, anxiety, loss, envy etc. Aristotle in "The Nicomachean Ethics" says, "Anyone can become angry, that is easy. But, to be angry with the right person to the right degree at the right time for the right purpose and right way - that is not easy".

Emotional Brain

Anger is a reaction, so the cause lies outside the system. Hence, choice is ours tool - to act or to react. Blind fury is a reaction. But, mild, modified tempered feelings of anger are an action.

According to Dr. Julie Fitness, Head of Department of Psychology at Macquarie University, Anger is perhaps one of the six hard-wired systems. Threats, irritations, shame, a sense of injustice, humiliation, embarrassment - all these arouse anger. When we feel slighted, we react. Some people know, to control the anger and behave in a very diplomatic way; some do not have this art.

It is proved that there is a part in the brain, in the prefrontal area that responds very rapidly to anger, within 200 milliseconds. Amygdala, which is called the emotional brain also, contributes its share here. Activity in the prefrontal area will be seen, when we are trying to regulate our anger responses. Professor Ray, from Department of Psychology and social behavior, UCLA, says, Anger is triggered by perceived threats to our interests. There is a strong connection between Amygdala and the prefrontal brain. We use these connections to regulate or control our responses in the Amygdala via the prefrontal cortex. Professor Ray, however, says that responses to anger, occurs throughout the body and it is quite individualistic. So, it depends on our personality, environment, our history and also our biology. When anger is aroused, the message from the emotional brain reaches the limbs through neurons in the brain .Our muscles twitch, sometimes stomach becomes upset, we feel pain in the lower back, heart rate goes high, BP goes high, shoulders experience pain etc. We have seen toddlers and preschool children putting up temper tantrums like biting, hitting, kicking etc. Handling anger is very important in preschool children. In fact, I would say, teaching children how to identify that they are angry and how to express their anger is very important. It is just unreasonable and impossible to expect young children, to be always calm, cool and composed. If we expect them to control their anger always, it may result in fear and anxiety, says Dr. Landy. Violence has at last, come to Indian schools also. It is observed that, children who grow with violence at home learn to be violent. In a recent study which concluded after 50 years of research, on the impact of violence in the media on children by L Rowell Huesmann of the University of Michigan and his colleague Brad Bushman, they state that exposure to violent electronic media has a larger adverse impact on children . Huesmann says that children spend an average of 3 hrs watching television each day and more than 60% of the TV programmes, contains some violence, including 40% showing extreme violence. Children who are living in communities that are racked by crime, religious fanaticism, menaced by friends and gangs who talk about violence always, tend to be violent. Children become violent and aggressive at home, because they lack trust in adults. They feel that they may not get consistent support from their family. This leads to some children primarily adolescent children, being physically violent. They indulge in destructive activities. Some of the worst aspects of anger, results out of mixed aggression and a feeling of deprivation. Anger is the most common feeling experienced by all. Usually we attribute our anger to others, friends, co-workers or bosses.

Is anger all that bad?

Professor Ray continues to say that, we cannot forget that anger is also the catalyst for some radical changes in the society like feudalism, slavery etc. Sometimes, when you are very angry you tend to work more, because it is so energizing and you feel more in control of the situation. It is a nicer feeling than feeling depressed, says Julie Fitness. Hence, anger cannot be always considered as a negative emotion. It is the consequences of anger that has to be adjusted or adapted or made functional or constructive. If we had not been angry, at social injustice, there wouldn't have been any reform in this world. There would not have been any necessity for court, law, justice etc. There has not been any proven record of gender differences in anger. Only the expression of anger differs. Women tend to cry when frustration occurs, whereas men try to retaliate. Some take revenge as a means to show their displeasure. This is the common phenomenon observed. We get angry not because something happens; we get angry because of what it means to us. Anger by itself, is not a problem, it becomes a problem, when its frequency, intensity, its duration and its modes of expression exceeds appropriate levels, says Dr. Ray. In western countries, violence in schools and colleges has become a frequent phenomenon. Why? Do the adults have anything to say?

In schools, handling children who are aggressive is a real art. In many cases, teachers are not exposed to this art and therefore the **interventions** may not always be successful. Today's teachers also are from the modern generation of impatience and quick money and so understanding children with compassion and empathy is lacking. The teacher training colleges have a major responsibility in sending out very responsible and compassionate human beings as teachers to the society. As they are handling living souls, they have to be extremely cautious. If any incorrect intervention happens, that may spoil the future of the children also.

Home, School, Community

All the above cases, reveal beyond doubt, how important is the home-school-society relationship in the development of children. Mental health of children particularly adolescents is a neglected area today because of a lack of understanding by adults. Aristotle says that "Even an embryo in the womb has an urge to evolve". The great French philosopher Henry Bergson says, that there is an Élan vital in every individual. This élan vital otherwise known as the intellectual energy helps an individual to evolve. Jainism, talks about a concept of "Anantaveerya - an inner energy". While all of them speak about the same fact i.e. evolution of an individual, it is very sad to note that, we adults refuse to understand and accept the inner urge of children to grow. While a certain influence on bringing up of children by parents is welcome, disrespecting the genuine urge of children to grow independently by them, has to be curbed. A certain amount of value systems at home is very important and values can never be taught and so, they have to be imbibed. If the values like truth, love, honesty, peace, compassion, empathy are to be developed in children, the same have to be practiced at home by adults. Are we doing that? May be in very few homes! We seek respect but do we give it to others? We, without hesitation, send the old people to old age homes! We expect our children to learn values and we expect the schools should teach them values because we are paying huge money as school fees.

Education today has become a commercial activity and higher versions of school education are available at a higher price. It is a widely accepted notion among parents that quality education comes only at a higher price and once they have done this duty of theirs, the onus of bringing up their children is entirely on the school. The school on the other hand places a lot of emphasis on academic performance only, losing out on human values. This conflict of interest between home and school, results in negligence of proper development in children. When children are expected to perform beyond their capabilities without giving them enough space to grow, they resort to violence, aggressiveness, humiliation and even sometimes, rejection of the self. The result is low self-esteem in at least some of the children where there is no family support.

In the recent times, we have been constantly hearing about different forms of punishment being meted out by teachers. We have also seen children resorting to violence and in many cases, even suicide attempts. Fear of failure, low self-esteem, peer pressure, high parental expectations are some of the reasons which cause anger among children. This hampers the development of their personality.

How Does Anger Affect Learning?

When children have drained out all their energy in showing anger, or warding off their own fears- they have difficulty in learning also [Craig (1992)].Distorted memories, discontinuous thought, impatience and suppressing the feelings are some of the factors that are seen as impediments in the learning process. It is proved that repressing these feelings can lead to health problems. Not all children retaliate to situations with resilience. When they have a nurturing family of adults, they learn to cope with the pressure. The others fall prey to anger!

How Can Schools Help in Anger Management?

The school curriculum today has to cater only to three Rs "Reading, writing and arithmetic". I would recommend a fourth R to be included which is "Emotional literacy", this will help the children to deal with emotions, moral views and value systems. This will comprise of life skills and social skills of problem solving, co-operation, tolerance, empathy, compassion and listening. This course would enable the children to have a personal identity, raise their self-esteem and achieve self-control. A framework of the module for this course is discussed as under:-

The Module of "Emotional Literacy"

The following module gives the outline as to how a curriculum can be built on emotional literacy in ordinary classrooms.

1. The teacher divides the children into five or six groups each comprising of a minimum of 5 children.
2. Each group brings up one case for discussion on any emotion particularly aggression and anger. They can draw, paint or put up posters on each case thereby expressing the anger or emotion.
3. The groups discuss and question each other on the cases explained. Each group brings out suggestions on three components 1) Stop- "I am feeling frustrated". 2) Think - "What can I do about it" 3) Reflect - "Which is the best thing to do?"
4. The teacher distributes worksheets based on the three components.
5. The teacher and the groups arrive at concept formulation- to suggest ways and means to handle each situation that was discussed by the groups.
6. Idea development- for emotional management- particularly anger and aggression management.

It is very important that the schools should not make it as an examining subject. If they do so, like what they have done now with value education, then, the worth is lost. The teacher has to formulate some rules and regulations before she/he starts this module and the rules should be pertaining to the time factor on each topic of discussion, allowing every member freedom to speak, controlling the impatience that may arise when disagreement between members emerge, not to mention names and learn to laugh at even on oneself. At least once a month a module on a particular emotion would add a lot to the emotional hygiene of the school.

Conclusion with an Appeal

The teachers of the school should get a training session by learned professors in psychology from the universities, on "Anger Management". This, not only helps the individual teacher in his /her life, but also helps to guide the students. The B. Ed. Training colleges should include "Emotional Literacy" as a module.

The topic on Learning difficulties has gained momentum in the last few years and the parents have learnt about their rights started asking for favours for waiving certain subjects for their children. The same wave that took over the education world should surge now in making emotional literacy as a part of the curriculum. How long can we wait for someone to take the lead?

I quote Khalil Gibran "Your children are not your children. They are the sons and daughters of Life's longing for itself. They came through you but not from you and though they are with you yet they belong not to you".

2

Perceptions and Perspectives on Anger and Development of Children

Dr. K.B. Kushal

George Bernard Shaw wrote: *"People are always blaming their circumstances for what they are. The people who get on in this world are the people who get up and look for the circumstances they want, and if they can't find them, make them."*

The development of the child depends to a significant extent on the manner in which anger is managed in his surroundings. Surroundings include the 16-odd hours the child spends in his home with parents living either as nuclear families or as joint set-ups. The remaining 8 hours of the day are spent in school and with peers. Psychologists and psychiatrists will testify to the fact that hatred begets hatred, anger begets anger and in establishments (establishments include institutions like school and home) where anger is controlled through validated processes and procedures- many of these being proven for their efficacy and potency for millennia by our sages and spiritual guides- the observers (children) actually show holistic development with high scores on social and spiritual quotients. On the other hand are children nurtured in establishments where anger is not only perceptible and discernible, but also visible to the impressionable mind of the child. Such children develop neurotic tendencies, end up as incomplete human beings, face relationship problems later in life and at times become a menace to self and society. Thus, for the healthy development of the child, it is necessary for all those interacting and dealing with the subject (child) on a daily basis, not only to ensure an anger-mitigated environment, but also to counsel and guide the child as to how to react when anger tends to overwhelm him. Unless the care-takers of the child are aware of the strategies to control and overcome anger, they can do little to prevent the child from becoming a victim of anger-related disorders. This paper, based upon the author's practical experience at dealing with anger during the various roles he has been playing as professor, Principal, parent, educationist and problem-solver, presents some practical strategies on anger management. These tips can be easily put to practices by any parent, teacher, counselor engaged in the mission of child development.

Anger

Anger is experienced as a turbulence, located in the overlapping frames of mind and heart. Anger is a strong reaction categorized as a negative emotion leading to imbalance and adversely impacting sane judgement. It's after-effects, created by residual streams of sentiments, linger long enough and affect the psychosomatic dimensions of personality. When the psychosomatic dimensions are impacted continually, disease is likely to follow in the form of chronic illnesses like blood-pressure, diabetes, migranes, epilepsy and many other prevalent disorders of modern times. It is now medically confirmed that anger produces hypertension, ulcers, palpitations, insomnia, fatigue. It breaks down relationships, interferes with communication, leads to guilt and depression. The recent instances of road-rage characterized by violent behavior exhibited by those on the driving seat of automobiles are a grim pointer to the extent to which the seeds of anger have embedded themselves in the psyche of people.

We have been advised in our religious, social and ethical

texts not to get angry i.e not to respond in a manner that is disproportionate to the situation. Lord Krishna says: "To the man who keeps on meditating on sense objects, there arises abundant attachment to them. From such attachment desire is born and from desire (when unfulfilled) springs anger all around. From anger comes great confusion (about right and wrong) and from this great confusion loss of memory. From loss of memory, there arises the destruction of the right disposition of the mind and from this destruction of intellect, he is lost and lost forever". Many Indian scriptures have spotted six evil tendencies that tempt and drag man downwards : Kama (Desire), Krodha (Anger) Lobha (Miserliness), Moha (Attachments) Madha (Infatuation and self deceit) and Matsarya (Intolerance, Jealousy). We can even say that Krodha and Lobha are but different manifestations of Kama. If what you desire is not secured, it leads to krodha; if you get what you desire, it leads to lobha.

At other times, anger is looked at as an expression of truthfulness, forthrightness, straight-forwardness, transparency, intolerance of inherent inconsistencies and serious moral breach. Ancient Rishis in India used to curse when they were angry, and offer boons when they were pleased. Jesus too had cursed a fig tree to be barren, and so it became so. The anger of Parshuram is legendary. King Sahastrarjun visited Jamadagni's place. There, he was lured by Kamdhenu cow and took her calf by force. When Parshuram learned about it, he punished the King and took his life. When King Sahastrarjun's son came to know about the incident, they retaliated. In the absence of Parshuram, they attacked and killed sage Jamadagni, Parshuram's father. This made Parshuram angry and he vowed to make the world void of kshatriyas. Parshuram, then executed every kshatriya from the face of the earth. Such was the anger of Parshuram.

Genesis of Anger

Anger is an immobilizing reaction, experienced when expectancy is not met. It takes the form of rage, hostility, striking out at someone or even glowering silence. It is an immobilization, wishing that the world and the people in it were different. In wishing that the world were different, the angry person is only displaying his emotional moral deficit leading to negative assertion. While positive assertive behavior is recommended and preferred, the tendency to get oneself judged on the basis of impulsive responses is something that is to be avoided at any cost. If emotional deprivation can be a cause for anger, the reverse is also true-surplus too can lead to anger. When anger arises due to surplus, one is actually celebrating his emotional hyper-positive assertion of personality. This indicates there is a heightened mental and emotional overflow in the person. In both the cases, there is lack of tolerance. There is loss of control over behavior and when you are not in control of your behavior, you are insane. Therefore, when you are angry and out of control, whether due to deficit, or due to surplus, you are temporarily insane. Anger arises if you are afraid of intimacy or love, you can get angry over something and thus avoid the risky business of sharing yourself affectionately.

Like all emotions, it is a result of thinking and perception variation arising from distortion, status-questioning and exaggeration. Annoyance, irritation, and disappointment are feelings that you will very likely continue to experience, since the world will never be the way you want it. But anger, that hurtful emotional response to obstacles, can be eliminated.

Strategies for Controlling Anger

Like other emotions, anger is an energy source and needs to be managed in the context of the situation. Many a time, anger has a reprimand value, a corrective value when delivered in incremental doses. Raising your voice to warn an erring child is perfectly justified. It only becomes anger when you are genuinely upset, when you get flushed and increase your heartbeat, when you slam things around and are generally immobilized for any period of time. You can raise your voice to demonstrate your strong feelings, but you should not go around being mad. While the provoker may act scared, he also knows that he can set the other person off whenever he wants, and therefore exercise the same kind of vindictive authority as the angry individual thinks he has. While teaching or counseling somebody, try faking anger. Raise your voice and look stern, but don't experience the physical and psychological pain that goes with anger. Remind yourself that you can dislike something without being angry about it.

You can become a witness (sakshi) to everything that is going within you. You work and think at the same time while a portion of your mind stands by and sees what you are thinking. The powers of the mind should be concentrated and turned back upon itself and as the darkest places reveal their secrets before the penetrating rays of the sun, so will this concentrated mind penetrate its own innermost secrets. Once Valmiki and his disciple Bharadraja went to bathe in the river. After Valmiki took his bath, he saw a male and female bird sitting in a tree. A hunter struck the male bird with his bow, killed him, and the bird fell out of the tree. Valmiki became angry and spontaneously cursed this hunter, "How cruel you are! How could you do this? May all your happiness go away, and may you never be happy again in your life." When Valmiki returned to his ashrama, he thought, "Why did I become so angry? I am supposed to be a rishi and have control over my senses. Life and death are very temporary, so why did I get disturbed seeing this? And how did these particular words come out of my mouth?" The moral of the story is that you can become a sakshi through reflective behavior, something which Valmiki did when he repented his behavior. Reflection leads to calming down and soothing of frayed nerves. Anger is a choice as well as a habit. Like all emotions, it is a result of thinking. Annoyance, irritation, and disappointment are feelings that you will very likely continue to experience, since the world will never be the way you want it. But anger, that hurtful emotional response to obstacles, can be eliminated through reflective behavior and realizing that it is you alone who can choose to be angry or not. First and most important, get in touch with your thoughts at the time of your anger, and remind yourself that you don't have to think that way, simply because you've always done so in the past. Awareness is paramount.

Anger is not an emotion that just **happens** to you. Anger is the reaction you **choose** to have. Events do not make you unhappy. It is your reaction to each event, your thoughts about it, that makes you unhappy. When confronted with people or events, which provoke you to choose anger, become aware of what you are telling yourself, and then work at new sentences, which will create new feelings and more productive behavior. Watch every word that you utter. Negative words block the flow of positive thoughts and words. The elimination of negative speech prepares your mind to receive the infinite wisdom to flow toward you. Darkness is a condition caused by the absence of light. The moment you bring a candle into a dark room, the darkness is dispelled. Similarly, when you use positive words, there is no room for negative words to thrive in your mind. Frequent use of positive words will eventually saturate your mind with positive infusion so that even the tendency for negative words will be uprooted from the spheres of your mind. You feel what you think, and you can learn to think differently about anything- if you decide to. Ask yourself if there is a sufficient payoff in being unhappy, down, or hurt. Then begin to examine, in depth, the kind of thoughts that are leading you to these debilitating feelings.

And the best way of bringing a candle in your dark room is to infuse the mind with folklore and stories from the puranas, panchatantra, upanishadas and other epics. Stories have proved to be the greatest behavior-changing resource. The story of the old fool who saw blood on his pet mongoose' mouth and, incensed at the thought that the animal had killed his son, pounded the faithful mongoose to death, only to realize and repent later that it was the other way round- the mongoose has actually protected the son against being stung by a deadly cobra – will stay forever in our minds, reminding us of what the scriptures and Lord Krishna have said millennia ago- *from this destruction of intellect, he is lost and lost forever.*

3

A Path towards Healing
Children Coping within a Hostile Environment

Christopher J. Rybak and Rebecca Earhart

Anger is a universal human reaction to one's environment under stress. Anger can often be experienced in a healthy manner such as when it leads to appropriate "fight or flight" responses. However, when disruptive patterns begin to emerge, unhealthy violent behaviors may be elicited and chaos can ensue. This contributes to an unpredictable environment in which others become angry and react with their own violence or turn the violence inward upon themselves through self-destructive behaviors. When children are exposed to repeated anger, the long-term physical, emotional and behavioral effects can be unsettling. It is vital that young people learn strategies to cope within a hostile environment. In the East, traditional techniques were developed such as meditation and yoga to calm one's mind and heart. Western developed coping techniques include systematic desensitization and various approaches to biofeedback such as Heartmath. These activities can bring awareness to the psychological and physiological messages one's body is communicating in reaction to stressful conditions. Early intervention through stress reducing techniques supports the development of effective coping mechanisms by young people.

When stress occurs for individuals, strong emotional reactions commonly follow including anger (Children and

Rozman, 2003). One may learn various means of coping with strong inner reactions to a hostile environment, sometimes effective and sometimes maladaptive. Many times the reactive patterns to stress will be strongly influenced by the models one has been exposed to, particularly in early childhood. Some families teach children to attend to their distress through naming the distress and talking about it with others. Other families teach more maladaptive reactions, such as aggressive reactions that often serve to exacerbate the difficulty and alienate others involved in the situation.

Along with happiness, sadness, and fear, anger is one of the primary emotions that link all human beings. In itself, the capacity to feel angry is healthy. Dr. Charles Spielberger, a psychologist who specializes in the study of anger, provides the following description, "anger is an emotional state that varies in intensity from mild irritation to intense fury and rage (APA, 2007). These intense, powerful, aggressive feelings can motivate humans to fight against harm or injustice and can be a productive emotion to bring about action. Although the literature reflects the notion that anger moves through human beings in the mind, body and spirit several competing theories regarding anger exist. For a number of cognitive-behavioral theorists (Beck, 2004; Ellis, 2001; Meichenbaum, 1977), anger begins as an internal cognitive process with a thought that triggers an angry feeling. This trigger thought might include a life stressor within the individual's environment or an idea or thought important to that person. Often humans feel angry before they are cognitively aware of the thought behind the anger. The body might become tense, with an increased heart rate and muscle tone (McKay, Fanning, Paleg, and Landis, 1996). Such angry thoughts and feelings leave an imprint on our soul.

On the other hand, theorists such as Sylvan Tomkins (1963), Carroll Izard (1991), and Paul Ekman and W.V. Friesen (1975) believed that affects such as anger are hard-wired into the connection between brain and facial expression. In other words, affect is primary and cognition of the anger follows the response to particularly evocative situations. For example, these theorists identified primary emotional reactions such as anger in the early development of infants long before there is clear evidence of cognitive processes such as appraisal of situations that might evoke anger reactions in more mature children and adults. As well, Goleman (2006) identified basic emotions such as joy, fear, and anger as "hardwired into the brain at birth." He saw the process of social development as involving both an increase in self-consciousness and an awareness of others and separate individuals from oneself. This enhancement of awareness of both self and other in relationship is the development of social intelligence.

Izard (1993) continued his research on the activation of emotion and identified four different levels of emotion activation, with three of the processes being non-cognitive and one cognitive, thus linking together the opposing views of emotion activation. The non-cognitive processes include *neural* activity such as changes in levels of neurotransmitters, *sensorimotor* activities include facial expression and posture, and *motivational* emotion activators include physiologically based drives such as hunger, fatigue, thirst, and sex. Izard saw each of these emotion activation processes as influencing cognitions and potentially having a recursive impact on one's emotional state.

In an angry environment, children's emotional states are effected differently because of their varying sensitivity to anger (McKay et al., 1996). Thus, some children are at decreased risk for maladjustment despite family conflict and stressful living conditions (Katz and Gottman, 1997). Positive parent-child relationships and peer relationships serve as protective factors for some children living in conflict (Katz and Gottman, 1997; Marcus and Betzer, 1996). Individual's who have certain protective factors may better able to incorporate effective coping skills into their life.

People use a wide range of coping skills to overcome their own or other's anger, such as breathing techniques, trusting dialogue, and exercise to release the feelings. Ayers,

Sandler, West and Roosa (1996) discussed coping under four factors: active coping, which includes problem solving and seeking understanding; social support such as emotion-focused support; distraction by action or physical release of energy; and avoidance either cognitively or behaviorally. Compas, Connor-Smith, Saltzman, Thomsen, and Wadsworth (2001) found that problem-focused and engagement coping were related with better adjustment compared to emotion-focused and disengagement. Deffenbacher, Lynch, Oetting, and Kemper (1996) suggested that cognitive-relaxation coping skills and social skills training were well-documented interventions to reduce anger in older adolescents. Levine (2000) identified five levels to managing anger including: 1) expression of anger to any provocation; 2) suppression of anger is learned; 3) acknowledgment of anger with direct expression; 4) no anger is necessary; 5) anger as a servant to appropriate action.

Certain research has explored the differences between coping strategies of females and males. Eschenbeck, Kohlmann, and Lohaus (2007) examined five subscales of coping, including seeking social support, problem solving, avoidant coping, palliative emotion regulation and anger-related emotion regulation and found that adolescent females more often seek social support and problem solve whereas boys of the same age are more likely to engage in avoidant coping. Goodwin (2006) found that female adolescents were more likely to pray, walk, talk with someone, argue or listen to music, while males of the same age were more likely to fight, bike, exercise, drink alcohol and use drugs. In general, an angry person, whether male or female, will typically express, suppress or calm in reaction to an angry internalized state (APA, 2007).

Anger and Development

According to psychologists specializing in this field, anger is both social and contextual. It is intended to produce action that leads to safety and security. However, if the angry feelings are not properly managed through coping skills, they can evolve into undesirable outcomes (DeAngelis, 2003). Ironically, two of the same reactions that can fulfill a productive immediate purpose, expressing and suppressing, can quickly manifest themselves in destructive ways. People who express their anger can quickly become violent and hostile towards their environment and those in it. Individuals who suppress their anger and turn inward can develop depression, anxiety and additional health problems (McKay et al., 1996; Verschuur, Eurelings-Bontekoe, and Spinhoven, 2004). Zeman, Shipman and Suveg (2002) found that adaptive coping with anger was inversely related to internalizing or externalizing symptoms.

Anger researchers explored the effects of diverting angry feelings, and they found when people try to hide their anger or irresponsibly project their anger they were at greater risk of anxiety, nervousness, tension and panic attacks (Cox, Bruckner, and Stabb, 2003). Studies have found that angry people often have a depleted immune system, and therefore become ill more frequently (Davis, 2000; Rein, Atkinson, and McCraty, 1995). In a more positive response, inducing one's own sense of compassion shows evidence of boosting the immune system (Rein et al., 1995).

When children are exposed to internal or external uncontrolled anger on a regular basis they are prone to experience a variety of health and emotional disturbances. As well, they are at risk to become emotionally stuck in an aggressive, depressive or anxious state. Unmanaged stress can cause long-term negative effects on many important areas of an adolescent's life, including social functioning (Hubbard and Coie, 1994), academic achievement (Deffenbacher et al., 1996) and physical health (Salovey, Rothman, Detweiler and Steward, 2000). Unmanaged anger contributes to dysfunctional relationships and such problems as bullying and other violence in schools (Deffenbacher, Oetting, and DiGiuseppe, 2002). When children routinely react with negativity including anger, other children identify the chronic negativity and notice the reduced relational ability of such children (Denham, 1998).

Studies show effects of anger on child development are destructive. Children are typically more aggressive and noncompliant (McKay et al., 1996). As well, young people experience poor overall adjustment and are less empathetic towards their fellow human. In general, angry environments can produce more delinquent children.

Children require external support for monitoring their emotions. Thus, it is vital for the well-being of the child that caregivers serve as appropriate role models in expressing their emotions as well as regulating the emotional experience of their children. Research conducted by Eisenberg, Fabes, and Murphy (1996) found that mothers who react to their children's negative emotional states in a manner that helps lessen the degree of negative arousal while fostering moderation in emotional expression is later correlated with more positive social functioning of the children. When this important modeling does not occur children can become ill equipped to handle the negative emotions they feel in a productive manner.

For preschool children, parents or surrogate parents greatly impact the manner in which children learn to process emotions. The ways in which parents model and encourage emotional expression greatly influence the development of children's emotional intelligence. Parents may harshly criticize anger, veer off into their own tirades, or calmly facilitate the child's beginning efforts to express and process difficult emotions such as anger (Denham, 1998). Children have been found to report anger, sadness, and fear in response to the expression of anger between adults in their presence. The correlation of negative emotional response was lessened when the anger resulted in partial or full resolution of a conflict (Cummins, Ballard, El-Sheikh, and Lake, 1991). Appropriate techniques such as conflict resolution can teach children effective ways to handle their own life stressors.

In general, children's acquisition of skill in regulating emotions is dependent on a complex interaction of inner personality factors and the socialization of emotional expression as experienced in the child's early formative years. The development of skills in emotional regulation can be derailed by inadequate parental emotional support, particularly when parental anger is misplaced toward the children through child abuse. Children who are themselves the direct recipients of harsh discipline by parents are more likely to act out in aggressive ways toward other children (Weiss, Dodge, Bates, and Pettit, 1992). Such aggressive actions were associated with a variety of impairments in social information processing including failure to pick up on relevant cues, a bias toward attributing hostile intent, an increased likelihood of choosing aggressive solutions to hypothetical problems, and tendency to anticipate positive outcomes to aggressive actions.

On the other hand, parents and other caregivers who identify and nurture emotional regulation by children help them to further their social development. The development of emotional competencies includes a range of skills including awareness, identification, and appropriate expression that often itself involves managing some degrees of discomfort and ambiguity as well as impulse control (Denham, 1998). Additional training methods for increasing the development of emotional and social intelligence and include managing anger and other difficult emotions are discussed next.

Paths toward Healing in Cultural Context

The social, contextual nature of anger makes it important to examine how young people around the globe cope with their angry environments or feelings. Coping includes attempting to regulate emotion, cognition, behavior, physiology and the environment as a response to stressful circumstances (Compas et al., 2001). Zeman and Shipman (1997) explored negative emotion in children and found that children report a greater inability to control anger, perhaps because they believe they lack the skills to mask anger. Researchers found that aggressive Chinese children who were taught anger coping methods and problem solving skills demonstrated less aggressive behaviors and changed their cognition regarding angry outbursts (Fung and Tsang, 2007). In Australia, researchers modeled and taught optimistic thinking skills to children who exhibited a greater level of control over their internal states and utilized fewer non-productive coping techniques (Cunningham, Brandon and Frydenberg, 2002).

In Great Britain, if children do not attain appropriate coping skills in the home, they are taught and reinforced in some classrooms. Burland (2006) uses visually stimulating material to suggest practical techniques students can learn and practice to manage their anger. Programs incorporating systematic desensitization have been utilized for children living within hostile environments in the United States (Ricci, 2006; Warren and McLellarn, 1982) and in South Africa (Akande, 2000). Researchers demonstrated that such techniques helped to decrease state anger, especially when coupled with a multifaceted approach of healing, including positive reinforcement, cognitive behavior modification, and use of fantasy and children's imagination.

Diong and Bishop (1999) conducted research with adults in Singapore regarding the relationship of anger expression, coping styles, and well-being. They found that active coping styles resulted in less expression of anger, lower levels of stress, and increased levels of physical and psychological well-being. In a study of highly angry Australian college students, Dua and Swinden (1992) found that interventions involving negative thought reduction, meditation, and even a placebo training treatment were each effective in reducing anger as a trait for the subjects.

In the U.S., a stress inoculation training program was found to be effective in reducing anger and aggression of incarcerated juvenile males (Schlichter and Horan, 1981). While the effectiveness of this training was demonstrated even with a challenging population, a number of subjects reported that newly developed positive the staff of the incarcerating institution actively ignored social skills. This suggests that further training in responding more effectively to the developmental level of the juveniles may be beneficial for institutional staff. Again this draws attention to the impact of the social intelligence level of parental figures and how their lacking of skills may potentially impede the development of youth in their charge.

Various cultures and traditions have given their own description to a path of healthy coping with the stress and distress of daily life. For example, the emotional strength through disciplined personal development of a Yaqui man of knowledge was originally recounted by Casteneda (1969) and later summarized by Globus and Globus (1983). At the center of this training is one finding "a path with heart" in which one learns to see everything as a challenge to achieve an exceptional level of well-being. Responding to anger inducing circumstances from this perspective allows one to advance one's emotional intelligence.

Mayan village culture developed a means to raise emotionally intelligent adolescents to a level of emotional eloquence, in which they could poetically describe the value, inner beauty, and social contributions of others to the group (Prechtel, 1999). Such emotionally eloquent individuals have a clear understanding of their participatory role in society and the connection they have with one's community. Having a larger sense of connection with the entire community provides a healthy context for adolescents to better understand the actions of others such that compassion otherwise upsetting actions may be responded to from a point of balanced emotional intelligence.

The Native American Medicine Wheel depicts a model of balance among the emotional, physical, spiritual, and intellectual realms of being (Coggins, 1990; Rybak, Lakota-Eastin, and Robbins, 2004). Developing such balance is an ongoing process that is based on awareness and gratitude toward what nature and life as a whole offers. The emphasis on understanding the greater context of the actions of others and responding from a point of being centered and balanced offers support toward greater compassion and less hostility.

In Buddhist tradition, anger is seen as a cause of suffering and that emotional reactions to events can be modified so that anger is managed in such a way as to minimize or eliminate suffering (Levine, 2000). While anger may be a part of the make up of a human being, so is the ability to change, adapt, and learn. The Buddhist practice of loving-kindness meditation or *Metta Bhavana* serves as a means of training oneself to develop positive emotional states of deep compassion toward all, starting with oneself, including those one respects highly, but also gradually moving to include those one may regard as rivals or even enemies (Dhammarakkhita, 2001). Once again, the emphasis of compassion over hostility encourages a positive emotional response to even difficult situations.

Based on the decidedly western technological approach to managing feelings, biofeedback programs such as Heartmath have been developed in order to assist individuals to monitor and adapt their emotional reactions to stressful situations, including anger (Childre and Rozman, 2003). Children with little emotional awareness are likely to internalize their feelings, and thus not access emotional support or act to change their environment (Zeman et al., 2002). Thus, in order to bring about positive change, it is important that young people understand and recognize their own emotions. Heartmath researchers have found a link between the type of heart rhythms and positive or negative emotional states. Negative emotions are associated with more chaotic heart rhythms while positive emotions are associated with coherent heart rhythms. Heartmath biofeedback technology is based on these associations, so that one can learn to recognize one's own state of coherence more fully as one more effectively manages one's emotional state. This type of biofeedback based on Heartmath has been used effectively with adults as well as children. Curriculum has been introduced into Western classrooms that bring focus to one's heart. Such practice has been shown to cut down learning issues and behavioral problems as well as reinforce healthier coping skills. One research study that incorporated elements of Heartmath along with training children other skills to improve emotional self-management showed significant improvements in managing anger and stress and in building relationship with others including family, teachers, and peers (McCraty, Atkinson, Tomasino, Goelitz, and Mayrovitz, 1999).

Discussion

Mayer and Salovey (1995) explored the connections between emotional intelligence and the ability to monitor and manage feelings. These authors described a high adaptation model of emotional regulation in which individuals learn that short-term pleasures are forgone for long-term pleasures. As well, they emphasize emotions that consider both individual and social interests, and recognize that the best emotions to feel in any given situation are according to the particular context, including the painful emotions.

Aspects of Mayer and Salovey's (1995) high adaptation model of emotional regulation differ primarily in terminology from concepts offered regarding the wisdom tradition of Tibetan Buddhism by the Dalai Lama in conversation with the psychiatrist Howard Cutler (1999). The Dalai Lama (1999) distinguished activities directed toward pleasure in the short-term from activities directed toward actual happiness in the long-term. Typically, activities that consider both the good of the individual as well as the good of others are more likely to lead to happiness, while short-term pleasure-producing activities are primarily for the individual's own indulgence and may have long-term negative consequences. The emphasis is on self-awareness and impulse control.

In addition to the paths toward healing described above, a variety of interventions have been developed toward improving the development of social and emotional intelligence. Denham and Burton (1996) developed a social-emotional intervention program for four year olds. The training emphasized building of relationships, increasing emotional awareness, and developing ways of solving interpersonal social problems. Children who had these interventions displayed increased social competence as compared to those who did not have the special training. Goleman (2006) outlined a number of case examples in which children, adolescents and adults who had once been caught up in a vicious spiral of anger and violence learned entirely new ways of relating to others, recognized the common humanity of others, and treated others with growing levels of compassion and social connection. Additional examples of research supporting these concepts were described above.

Anger management can be seen as an integral piece of the entire context of social and emotional development. Practical application utilizing techniques to manage anger have been used in clinical and educational settings. Adolescents who learn to identify internal and external triggers, maintain an anger log and enhance social supports have demonstrated less angry episodes within their environment. As well, adolescents evaluated others reactions to angry situations and experienced insight regarding appropriate and effective techniques to manipulate anger. At times anger can be expressed in quite appropriate ways, but so often children are not taught appropriate methods of managing and expressing anger. Such insight has helped adolescents find suitable role models in which to follow.

Taking a look at the flip side shifts our focus from the negative to the positive side of development. In his definition of social intelligence, Goleman (2006) identified two primary dimensions: social awareness and social facility. Social awareness includes the ability to express empathy toward others, attuning to others, and knowledge of how the social world functions. Social facility includes the ability to apply one's social awareness in effective interactions with others non-verbally, in social interaction, and acting with compassion. As previously discussed, behaving compassionately has a positive impact on self and others.

Conclusion

The continual cycle of anger, hostility, and violence perpetrated by adults on children, perpetuated by children on children, and then passed on to the next generation through the spread of yet more anger, hostility, and violence can be disrupted and healed through a variety of training methods. These training methods include enhancing the social and emotional intelligence of individuals through building a sense of empathic connection and relationship with others, heightening self-awareness, and fostering effective means of solving interpersonal problems. In addition, research suggests that including those who influence and serve as models to youth may enhance such training. A variety of culture-specific approaches to develop social and emotional intelligence based on the wisdom traditions of those cultures were described. In addition, a number of intervention approaches were described that are based on the developmental models evolving from current scientific research. With guidance and support, children can learn to feel anger and subsequently act with appropriate coping techniques in order to secure a more peaceful and centered place in the world.

REFERENCES

Akande, A. (2000). Effects of exposure to violence and poverty on young children: The southern african context. *Early Child Development and Care*, 163, 61-78.

American Psychological Association. (2007). *Controlling anger before it controls you.* Retrieved on November 4, 2007 from: http://www.apa.org/topics/controlanger.html

Ayers, T.S., Sandler, I.N., West S.G. and Roosa, M.W. (1996). A dispositional and situational assessment of children's coping: Testing alternative models of coping. *Journal of Personality*, 64, 923-958.

Beck, A.T., Freeman, A. and Davis, D. (2004). *Cognitive therapy of personality disorders (2nd Ed.)*. New York: Guilford Press.

Burland, R. (2006). *Successful anger management for young children.* Barnstaple: Chelfham Mill School Outreach Publications.

Casteneda, C. (1969). *The teachings of don juan: A Yaqui way of knowledge.* New York: Ballantine.

Childre, D., and Rozman, D. (2003). *Transforming anger: The Heartmath solution for letting go of rage, frustration, and irritation.* Oakland, CA: New Harbinger.

Coggins, J. (1990). *Alternative pathways to healing: The recovery medicine wheel.* FL: Health Communications.

Compas, B.E., Connor-Smith, J.K, Saltzman, H, Thomsen, A.H and Wadsworth, M.E. (2001). Coping with stress during childhood and adolescence: Problems, progress and potential in theory and research. *Psychological Bulletin,* 127, 87-127.

Cox, D., Bruckner, K., and Stabb, S. (2003). *The anger advantage.* New York: Broadway Books.

Cummins, E.M., Ballard, M., El-Sheikh, M. and Lake, M. (1991). Resolution and children's response to interadult anger. *Developmental Psychology, 27,* 462-470.

Cunningham, E.G., Brandon, C.M., and Frydenberg, E. (2002). Enhancing coping resources in early adolescence through a school-based program teaching optimistic thinking skills. *Anxiety, Stress and Coping: An International Journal,* 15(4), 369-381.

Davis, J.L. (2000). *Seeing red is bad for your health.* WebMD medical news. Retrieved on November 6, 2007 from: http://www.webmd.com/news/20000421/anger-health-effects.

DeAngelis, T. (2003). When anger's a plus: despite its mixed reputation, anger can play a constructive role at home, at work and in the national consciousness, psychologists are finding. *APA Monitor,* 34(3), 44.

Deffenbacher, J.L., Lynch, R.S., Oetting, E.R., and Kemper, C.C. (1996). Anger reduction in early adolescents. *Journal of Counseling Psychology.* 43(2), 149-157.

Deffenbacher, J., Oetting, E., and DiGiuseppe, R. (2002). Principles of empirically supported interventions applied to anger management. *The Counseling Psychologist, 30,* 262-280.

Denham, S. (1998). *Emotional development in young children.* New York: Guilford.

Denham, S., and Burton, R. (1996). A social-emotional intervention for at-risk 4-year-olds. *Journal of School Psychology, 34,* 225-245.

Dhammarakkhita, V. (2001). *Metta bhavana ~ Loving-kindness meditation.* Bangkok: Dhammodaya Meditation Centre.

Diong, S., and Bishop, G.D. (1999). Anger expression, coping styles, and well-being. *Journal of Health Psychology, 4,* 81-96.

Dua, J.K., and Swinden, M.L. (1992). Effectiveness of negative-thought-reduction, meditation, and placebo training treatment in reducing anger. *Scandinavian Journal of Psychology, 33,* 135-146.

Eisenberg, N., Fabes, R.A., and Murphy, B.C. (1996). Parents' reactions to children's negative emotions: Relations to children's social competence and comforting behavior. *Child Development, 67,* 2227-2247.

Ekman, P., and Friesen, W.V. (1975). *Unmasking the face.* Englewood Cliffs, NJ: Prentice-Hall.

Ellis, A. (2001). *Feeling better, getting better, staying better: Profound self-help therapy for your emotions.* Atascadero, CA: Impact Publishers.

Eschenbeck, H., Kohlmann, C., Lohaus, A. (2007). Gender differences in coping strategies in children and adolescents. *Journal of individual differences.* 28(1) 18-26.

Fung, A., and Tsang, S. (2007). Anger coping method and skill training for Chinese children with physically aggressive behaviors. *Early Child Development and Care.* 177(3), 259-273.

Globus, M., and Globus, G. (1983). The man of knowledge. In R. Walsh and D. Shapiro (Eds.) *Beyond health and normality: Explorations of exceptional psychological well-being.* New York: Von Norstrand Reinhold Co.

Goleman, D. (2006). *Social intelligence: The new science of human relationships.* New York: Bantam.

Goodwin, R.D. (2006). Association between coping with anger and feelings or depression among youths. *American Journal of Public Health, 96,* 664-669.

H.H. Dalai Lama, and Cutler, H. (1999). The art of happiness: A handbook for living. London: Hodder and Stoughton.

Hubbard, J.A. and Coie, J.D. (1994). Emotional correlates of social competence in children's peer relationships. *Merrill-Pulmer Quarterly*, 40, 1-20.

Izard, C.E. (1991). *The psychology of emotions.* New York: Plenum Press.

Izard, C.E. (1993). Four systems of emotion activation: Cognitive and noncognitive processes. *Psychological Review, 100,* 68-90.

Katz, L.F., and Gottman, J.M. (1997). Buffering children from marital conflict and dissolution. *Journal of clinical child psychology,* 26, 157-171.

Levine, M. (2000). *The positive psychology of Buddhism and yoga: Paths to mature happiness.* Mahway, NJ: Lawrence Erlbaum.

Marcus, R. F., and Betzer, P. D. S. (1996). Attachment and antisocial behavior in early adolescence. *Journal of Early Adolescence,* 16(2), 29-248.

Mayer, J.D., and Salovey, P. (1995). Emotional intelligence and the construction and regulation of feelings. *Applied and Preventive Psychology, 4,* 197-208.

McCraty, R., Atkinson, M., Tomasino, D., Goelitz, J., and Mayrovitz, H.N. (1999). The impact of an emotional self-management skills course on psychosocial functioning and autonomic recovery to stress in middle school children. *Integrative Physiological and Behavioral Science, 34,* 246-268.

McKay, M., Fanning, P., Paleg, K., and Landis, D. (1996) *When anger hurts your kids: A parent's guide.* MJF Books: New York.

Meichenbaum, D. (1977). Cognitive behavior modification: An integrative approach. New York: Plenum Press.

Prechtel, M. (1999). *Long life, honey in the heart.* New York: Tarcher.

Rein, G., Atkinson, M., and McCraty, R. (1995). The physiological effects of compassion and anger. *Journal of Advancement in Medicine, 8,* 87-105.

Ricci, L.L. (2006) Effects of cognitive restructuring with desensitization for anger reduction in adolescent boys. *Dissertation abstracts international: Section B: The sciences and engineering,* 67(1-B).

Rybak, C., Lakota-Eastin, C., and Robbins, I. (2004). Native American healing practices and counseling. *Journal for Humanistic Education and Development, 43,* 25-32.

Salovey, P., Rothman, A.J., Detweiler, J.B., and Steward, W.T. (2000). Emotional states and physical health. *American Psychologist,* 55, 110-121.

Schlichter, K.J., and Horan, J.J. (1981). Effects of stress inoculation training on the anger and aggression management skills of institutionalized juvenile delinquents. *Cognitive Therapy and Research, 5,* 359-365.

Tomkins, S. (1963). *Affect, imagery, and consciousness: Vol. 2. The negative affects: Anger and fear.* New York: Springer.

Verschuur, M., Eurelings-Bontekoe, E., Spinhoven, P. (2004) Associations among homesickness, anger, anxiety and depression. *Psychological Reports.* 94(3), 1155-1170.

Warren, R. and McLellarn, R. (1982). Systematic desensitization as a treatment for maladaptive anger and aggression: A review. *Psychological reports,* 50(3), 1095-1102.

Weiss, B., Dodge, K.A., Bates, J.E., and Pettit, G.S. (1992). Some consequences of early harsh discipline: Child aggression and a maladaptive social information processing style. *Child Development, 63,* 1321-1335.

Zeman, J. and Shipman, K. (1997) Social-contextual influences on expectancies for managing anger and sadness: The transition from middle childhood to adolescence. *Developmental Psychology.* 33(6), 917-924.

Zeman, J., Shipman, K., and Suveg, C. (2002). Anger and sadness regulation: Predictions for internalizing and externalizing symptoms in children. *Journal of Clinical Child and Adolescent Psychology, 31,* 393-398.

4

HELPING YOUNG CHILDREN TO MANAGE WITH ANGER

Dr. S. Jaya

A study was conducted on "helping young children to manage with anger" with 50 selected children aged 7-12 years to find out anger provoking situations at school and home. The parents and teachers of the children were also selected. The children became angry when their activities were interrupted and when they were criticized by gang members constantly. Unfavorable comparisons, non-cooperation of friends, unnecessary punishment and violent computer/video games were the few causes for anger provoking situations. The parents could identify the signs of anger with their children, could give better responses for anger situations, instilled anger management exercises and directed children to think in a positive way. Sometimes they left their children to relax and altered their activities. Teachers of the selected children could help them to deal with anger by guiding them. They practiced to give a safe emotional atmosphere in the class, looked after their needs then and there and counseling children in a positive way.

Anger is a fundamental emotion and not a behavior. It is normal experienced by everyone, and it is manageable. It serves as our instinctual and natural "flight or flight" protection. It is a fact that children become angry both in school and at home. In early childhood, children begin to master the ability to suppress physically aggressive impulses (pushing, hitting, pinching, biting, yelling) when they are angry. Preschool-aged children are learning to identify basic emotional states in themselves and others with the use of words. However, it is common to see young children resort to physically acting out behaviors (throwing toys, pushing or hitting a parent or peer) as they are still becoming accustomed to using words to express their feelings.

As children age, they develop more sophisticated language skills and begin to be able to take the perspective of others. They develop empathy and are better able to understand the effect of their actions and words have on others. By the later elementary grades, children should be able to express angry feelings verbally as opposed to physically. However, children with language difficulties or difficulties controlling impulses frequently struggle with managing angry feelings and may resort to physically acting out, yelling, or refusing to obey school or household rules.

The way children expresses anger is learned from parents, other family members, friends, community and media. The natural way to express anger is to respond with aggression. It is the instinctive response to believed physical or verbal threats. Responding aggressively in every threatening situation, however, is not healthy or safe. Aggressive acts can lead to social problems, difficulties with family members, troubles with the law, and physical or emotional harm. Therefore, it is important that children, at an early age, are taught effective, healthy ways of controlling their anger.

The Emotional State of Anger

- The first component is the emotion itself- a feeling experienced when a goal is blocked or needs is frustrated. The following are the possible causes / stress producing anger provocations that young children face daily in classroom interactions. (Marion, 1997).
- Conflict over possessions (taking or contending over property or space),

- Physical assault (harsh physical contact with others, such as pushing, hitting, or fighting),
- Verbal conflict (teasing, taunting, or arguing),
- Rejection (being ostracized from peers or being ignored by those in authority), and
- Issues of compliance (involving, asking or insisting that children conform to Standard that may not be what they want to do).

Expression of Anger

The second component of anger is its expression, some children express anger through facial expressions, crying, sulking, or talking, but do little to try to solve a problem or confront the provocateur. Others actively resist by physically or verbally defending their positions, self esteem or possessions of non aggressive ways. Still other children express anger with aggressive revenge by physically or verbally retaliating against the provocateur. Some other children express anger through avoidance or attempts to escape from or evade the provocateur. And some children use adult seeking, looking for comfort or solutions from a teacher, or telling the teacher about an incident.

An Understanding of Anger

The third component of anger experience is understanding - interpreting and evaluating - the emotion. Because the ability to regulate the expression of anger is linked to an understanding of the emotion and because children's ability to reflect on their anger is somewhat limited, children need guidance from teachers and parents in understanding and managing their feelings of anger.

The following are some possible signs of difficulty coping with anger:

- Fear of being out of control when you are angry
- Often feel tense, irritable or frustrated?
- Find yourself frequently gossiping or complaining about

others rather than speaking to them directly about what is bothering you?

- Frequently feel hurt or resentful that others treat you unfairly
- Take out your anger on someone or something else rather than the person or situation that is bothering you
- Physically lashed out when angry (eg. destroyed property, hit someone etc).

Explosion of Anger

Everyone can identify the explosive personalities. They usually yell, scream, wave their arms, seethe, breath hard and otherwise call attention to them. However, children who suppress their feelings are difficult to identify. They appear passive and hardly exhibit any emotions. Here are a few medical/physical manifestations of students who suppress their anger.

Frequent headaches (medical attention has ruled out any physical disorder as the cause),

- Gastrointestinal disorders,
- Respiratory disorders,
- Skin disorders (hives),
- Arthritis,
- Disabilities of the nervous system,
- Aggravation of existing physical symptoms,
- Emotional disturbances, and
- Suicide.

Aggressive or passive behavior disrupts the academic environment. When teachers are confronted with either behavior, the safe and orderly learning environment of the school is at risk. Students deserve the opportunity to learn appropriate ways to express anger effectively and appropriately.

Educators, parents and others reduce the chance of violence in our children and youth when we give them the ability to arrive at nonviolent solutions to problems by teaching those skills.

With this background the investigator has taken up the study to,

- Find out the causes of anger among children in school and at home
- Find out the methods followed by the parents and teachers
- Find out the impact of counseling skills developed among the selected teachers.

Methodology

The investigator selected late childhood period with the age group from 7 – 12 years as the respondents for her study. Twenty-five boys and girls were selected from two schools. Interview schedule and Questionnaires were framed to collect information from the students, teachers and parents separately. The researcher was so curious to find out the causes for anger. Hence anger provoking situations in classrooms, home, and the responsibility of parents and teachers to control anger were included in the interview schedule. The investigator collected information individually.

Findings of the Study

The findings of the study are presented under the following headings such as

- Anger provoking situations in class rooms
- Anger provoking situations at home
- Symptoms of hidden anger
- Methods followed by the parents and children.
- Methods developed among teachers to control children's anger.

Anger provoking situations in classrooms

The investigator tried to find out the situations, which provoke the respondents to get angry. The table 1 expresses the different situations in class rooms, which created anger among the children.

TABLE - 1
Anger Provoking Situations in Class Rooms

N: 25

S.No	Causes	Boys (%)	Girls (%)
1.	Interruption in interested activities	90	86
2.	Constant criticism by gang members and others	88	82
3.	Unfavorable comparisons	86	62
4.	Non-cooperation of friends and classmates	80	78
5.	Coming late to School	72	52
6.	Lack of time to do homework	62	46
7.	Inability to understand teaching	60	58
8.	Blocking of desires to share in the activities	54	56
9.	Inability to cope up learning	52	46
10.	Type of discipline followed in the School	50	45

Children became angry when their activities were interrupted (B: 90% G: 86%), criticised by the gang members and others constantly (B: 88% G:82%)and during unfavorable comparisons with other children (B:86% G:62%). Eighty percent of the boys and 78 percent of girls induced to get anger by non-cooperation of the friends and classmates. Seventy-two and 54 percent of both boys and girls were disturbed and got anger when they were disturbed in which they were interested. Non-cooperation of their friends motivated these children (B:72% and G: 68%) to get anger enormously. Seventy two percent of boys and 52 percent of girls got anger, when they were late to school.

Lack of time to do homework was the basis for anger to 62 percent of boys and 46 percent of girls. Inability to understand the teaching in class rooms made 60 percent and 58 percent of the boys and girls to get anger. In general more boys got anger for different causes than girls. Blocking of desires, inability to cope up learning and the type of discipline followed in the school were the other reasons mentioned by nearly half of the respondents.

Anger provoking situations at home

The selected children were asked to express the reasons for their anger at home. Table 2 gives the reasons for the respondent's anger at home.

TABLE - 2

Anger Provoking Situations at Home N: 25

S.No	Causes	Boys (%)	Girls (%)
1.	Conflicts over routine physical habits	92	54
2.	Sibling Rivalry	86	84
3.	Denial of attention and negligence by family members	76	64
4.	When the needs and wants are not fulfilled	76	86
5.	Unreasonable comparison with other children	78	62
6.	When people are sarcastic	74	62
7.	Conflicts with family members	64	62
8.	When the privileges are refused	64	82
9.	Violent computer games	62	-

More number of (92%) of the boys experienced anger as they had conflicts over routine habits than girls (54%). Sibling rivalry was also observed among the majority of the selected children (boys: 86 %, girls: 84 %) irrespective of the sex. Denial of attention and negligence by the family members was one of the reasons to get anger is depicted by 76 and 64 percent of both boys' girls respectively. When the needs and wants were not fulfilled properly 76 percent of the boys and 86 percent of the girls experienced anger at home. Unfavorable comparisons with older children forced 78 percent of the boys and 62 percent of the girls to get angry at home. Seventy four percent of the boys and 62 percent of the girls felt anger when people behaved sarcastically with them. It is clear that the girls (82%)

were highly sensitive when their privileges were denied than the boys (62%). Sixty-four and 62 percent of boys and girls had conflicts with their family members, which provoked them to get anger. Violent computer games generated 62 percent of boys, whereas none of the girls played violent games as they are not interested.

Symptoms of hidden anger

Sometimes the children tend to hide their anger. Table 3 depicts hidden symptoms/signals that negative feelings are bottled up in children.

TABLE - 3

Symptoms of Hidden Anger N: 50

S.No	Symptoms	Boys (%)	Girls (%)
1.	Frequent disturbing or frightening dreams	86	64
2.	Clenched jaws-while sleeping	86	42
3.	Grinding of teeth, chronically stiff neck	84	40
4.	Difficulty in getting sleep	72	69
5.	Loss of interest in enthusiastic activities	72	74
6.	Smile while hurting	36	76
7.	Getting tired more easily than usual	44	64

Frequent disturbing or frightening dreams were one of the most important hidden symptoms among boys (86%) than girls (64%). As boys are stronger, naturally majority of them (86%) clenched their jaws while sleeping and grinded their teeth chronically and had stiff neck (84%) while hiding their anger than girls (40%). An average of 70 percent of both boys and girls had difficulty in sleeping and lost their interest in enthusiastic activities. Majority of the girls (76%) could control their anger and showed smile when somebody hurt them than boys (36%) as they are aggressive in nature. More easily both boys (44%) and girls (64%) displayed their tiredness than usual.

Methods followed by the parents and teachers

The parents of the selected children were approached to give their methods to reduce the anger of their children. Table 4 represents the practices adopted by the parents and teachers.

TABLE - 4
Methods Followed by the Parents and Teachers

N: 50

S.No	Practices Adopted	Boys (%)	Girls (%)
Parents			
1.	Recognized Childs anger	86	84
2.	Gave better responses to anger situations	84	82
3.	Instilled anger management exercises	78	15
4.	Diverted their children to think in a positive way	64	56
5.	Satisfying child's needs	60	44
6.	Encouraging children to express out	60	50
7.	Cultivating sense of humor	46	60
8.	Left children to relax and altered them with some other activities	48	68
Teachers			
1.	Secured emotional atmosphere in the class	80	86
2.	Looked after their needs then and there	74	84
3.	Counseling children in a positive way	60	68

Majority of the parents (B: 86% G: 84%) could identify their child's' anger and could give better responses to anger situations. Nearly three fourth of the boys (78%) were given anger management exercises, whereas only very few of the parents of the girls (15%) implemented the same and diverted their children to think in a positive way (B: 64% G: 56%). Sixty and 44 percent of the parents of both boys and girls satisfied their children's need after seeing their mood and encouraged children to express their feelings. Forty six and

68 percent of the parents of both boys and girls cultivated a sense of humor, when children were in anger mood. More parents of the number of girls could develop humor among girls than boys.

Majority of the teachers developed a safe emotional atmosphere in a class, looked after children's needs then and there, and counseled children in a positive way

Methods developed among teachers to control anger

The selected teachers were given counseling for a period of one month and this method was found to be successful to manage children's anger. The details are given in the table 5.

TABLE - 5

Impact of Counseling Skills Adopted by the Teachers to Control Children's Anger

N: 50

S.No	SKILLS DEVELOPED	Percentage
1.	Recognize stress	100
2.	Develop Empathy	100
3.	Respond instead of react	100
4.	Communicate assertively	100
5.	Develop forgiveness	100

Stress and anger tend to go hand and hand. The higher the stress level, it is easier to allow our anger to get out of control. Hence the teachers of the selected respondents were given counseling to handle anger situations. All of them could recognize the stress situation and developed their empathy level. All the respondents could respond politely and calmly instead of reacting immediately and aggravate children more towards anger. The teachers developed the nature of forgiveness and could communicate assertively.

Conclusion

Teachers, parents and adults have important roles in the

lives of children and adolescents. They should have enough knowledge about proper management to guide angry children. Anger becomes more complex as it develops over the years. It can be manifested in many ways and fused with other emotions, if never appropriately managed; anger may be destructive to the child's psychological and physical well-being.

Recommendations

The following are the recommendations for the teachers and parents:

Teacher's role in helping children to manage their anger

Anger management is a skill that students can learn. It is merely a brief catalog of common sense behaviors and strategies that teachers and other adults can use to develop anger management skills in children. Educators should, always remember that emotions are triggers that incite anger, and the keys to individual responses to anger and its control are unique to each particular child.

Create a safe emotional climate – Teachers should create a classroom with clear, consistent, and flexible boundaries, one in which every student is treated fairly and is subject to consistent enforcement of a set of rules known and respected by everyone.

Help children develop self-regulatory skills – Self-control and reflection skills allow children to regulate their own behavior.

Encourage children to label their feelings – usually a feeling precede an angry response. It may be frustration, embarrassment, shame, or any number of triggers. If children learn to identify their feelings that precede reactions, their ability to exercise self-control will grow.

Use books and stories about anger to help young children understand and manage anger – there are many books for young children that can help validate their feeling and educate them as to what is taking place inside them.

Communicate with parents – Educators should share with parents what is being done to teach children to manage anger. Such efforts are much more likely to be successful if parents model the appropriate skills and reward responsible behavior in their children.

Parent's role in helping children to manage their Anger

Help them identify the early warning signs of anger – Learn to recognize the cues that your child is begging to get frustrated. Look for signs that come before the eruption. Once you know the cues begin to point them out to your child. Make observation and teach your child to recognize those signs. Eventually children will be able to move from the emotion to the right action, they must be able to recognize the cues that anger is intensifying.

Step back:

Teach your child to take a break from the different situation and to get alone for a few minutes. During that time the child can rethink the situation, calm down and determine what to do next. Stepping back can help the child stop the progression and determine to respond differently.

Choose a better response – After the child has stepped back and settled down, then it's time to decide more appropriate response to the situation. There are three positive choices

- talk about it
- get help or
- slow down but keep at it

Simplifying the choices makes the decision process easier. Even your children can learn to respond constructively to frustration when they know there are choices. These choices are actually skills to be learned. Take time to teach your children these skills and practice them as responses to angry feelings.

Encourage them to talk it out

Children feel better when they talk about their feeling

or lift the burden of having to face their fears alone and offer an emotional release. If your child appears constantly depressed, angry or upset, it is especially important to reassume him and encourage him to talk about his concerns. Let him understand anger is a normal emotion. However acting out anger, hurting others and uncontrolled anger is not okay.

Help them find an outlet

We all need on outlet to vent our emotion before they build into an eruption. Sports or physical activity is a great way for kids to burn off that energy. Other kids might prefer to write out their feelings. Soft, relaxing music be another alternative to help those angry feelings.

Monitor the media

Pay special attention to the kinds of media your children play with or watch. Over the years, many experts have concluded that viewing a lot of violence in the media can be risky for children. It is true that watching too much violence whether on TV, in the movies, or in video games can increase the chance that children would be desensitized to violence or even act more aggressively then.

Control your own behavior

When it comes to learning how to behave, children often follow their parents' lead, which is why it is important to examine how you approach conflict. Do you use violence to settle arguments? When you are angry, do you yell or use physical force? If you want your child to avoid violence, show the right behavior for her, realize and she will imitate your responses and reactions.

Help them see how others feel

Children and adolescents struggle when it comes to understanding the feeling of others. One of the most important things you can do, as a parent is to help instill a sense of empathy. The ability to identify with and understand the feelings of another. Many times, young people lash out in an attempt to feel better but do not realize they hurt those around them.

Never try to reason with a child who is enraged

Sometimes children become enraged. The primary way to tell when children are enraged is that they can no longer think rationally and their anger is now controlling them. Unfortunately, many parents try to talk their children out of anger, often leading to more intensity whether it is the two year old temper tantrum or the 14 years old ranting and raving, do not get sucked into dialog. It only escalates the problem. Talking about it is important but wait until after the child has settled down. Leave the room and tell the child when they want to "try again" to come talk. Do not leave in anger or defeat.

REFERENCES

American Psychological Association. *Controlling Anger-Before it Controls You.* Retrieved December 2000, from the World Wide Web: www.helping.apa.org/daily/anger.html.

Marion, Marian. (1997). *Helping Young Children Deal With Anger.* Retrieved December 2000, from the World Wide Web: www.ed.gov/databases/ERIC_Digests/ed414077.html. University of Cincinnati. (1997-2000).

Some Facts Psychologists Know About...Anger. Retrieved December 2000, from the World Wide Web, www.psc.uc.edu.

5

Relationship between Self-Identity Styles, Self-Assertiveness and Self-Efficacy among Adolescents

Leila Piri

The purpose of this study was to investigate the relation between ego identity styles self- assertiveness and self-efficacy of male junior university students in Pune. one-hundred and twenty-four participants completed Berzonsky's Identity Style Inventory (1990), Townend's Assertiveness Questionnaire (1991) and Jerusalem and Schwarzer's General self efficacy scale (1992). Results showed that students who had the informational identity style had more self efficacy than the students who had normative identity style. There was no defuse/avoidance identity style among these students.

Results also indicated that the informational Identity style had a correlation of 0/30 with assertive behavior, and a correlation of 0/18 with passive behavior. The normative identity style had a correlation of 0/35 with passive behavior. The implications of using measures developed in individualistic cultures for more collective cultures is discussed. Also the variables are investigated in collective cultures like India.

Over the years, much research has been devoted to examining the personal and social determinants of successful development over the course of adolescence (Compas, Hinden, and Gerhardt,1995; Lerner and Steinberg, 2004). Adolescence involves the management of major biological, educational, and social role transitions that tend to occur concurrently. The success with which the challenges of these transitions are managed depends, to a large degree, on adolescents'ability to behave appropriately in multiple domains. Although most research has focused on the undesirable outcomes that may preclude healthy development (Cairns and Cairns, 1994; Cicchetti and Toth, 1998; Jessor, 1998), no less important are the positive outcomes and personal factors that allow young people to navigate safely through the challenges of adolescence and set a successful life course. Thus, the scientific study of adolescence needs to explain why some youth cope effectively with taxing role demands and interpersonal strains whereas others withdraw in the face of challenges and, ultimately, may succumb to unhappiness and depression.

In the present study, the ability to express oneself assertively and self-efficacy as perceived ability to produce a desired action as two important abilities for effective performance and their relationship with identity styles has been explored.

Self-assertiveness has been literally defined as "the tendency to express oneself which indicates fearless without needing to present any evidence or document" (Bower and Bower, 1978, p. 4). The notion of assertiveness has been broadened to include the expression of one's feelings, preferences, needs or opinions in a way which is neither threatening nor punishing toward another person, and does not involve an undue or excessive amount of anxiety or fear (Alberti and Emmons,1982; Galassi and Galassi, 1978; lazarus, 1973). Self-efficacy refers to the perceived ability to produce a desired action. Self-efficacy is more than telling ourselves that we can succeed; it is a strong conviction of competence that is based on our evaluation of various sources of information about our abilities (Bandura, 1986).

Different variables have been found to correlate with self-assertiveness and self efficacy. Some of these variables include culture (Schweder et al., 1997), gender and sexual identity (Renk and Creasey, 2003), Racial Identity (Kimberli,2001), level of education (Rodriguez, 2001), social support (Sheriden and Radmacher, 1992), and identity development (Persona and Persona, 1992), Anxiety (Chan,1993 and Muris,2001).

Identity is a conceptual structure composed of postulates, assumptions, and constructs relevant to the self interacting in the world (Berzonsky, 1993). Erickson (1968) posited ego identity as the personality component undergoing a time of special ascendancy during the adolescent years. He described ego identity as serving a variety of functions including sameness overtime, inner coherence, the synthesis of successive identifications, and protection against experiences of sudden discontinuities occasioned by biological development or changes in life circumstances.

Empirical research on Eriksons'theory of identity development has been guided by the identity status paradigm outlined by Marcia(1966). In his paradigm, identity development was thought to result from two basic underlying processes, namely, exploration and commitment. Exploration was defined as the degree to which an individual engages in a personal search for values, beliefs, and goals, and implies experimenting with different social roles, plans, and ideologies. Commitment refers to the determined adherence to a set of convictions, goals and values. Based on these dimensions, Marcia (1966) defined four identity statuses: achievement, moratorium, foreclosure, and diffusion. Marcia identity status paradigm focuses primary on the outcomes of the process of identity formation, that is, it describes identity mainly in terms of enduring outcomes and stable, dispositional characteristics (Cote and Levine, 1988; soenens, Duriez, Goossens, 2003).

A number of theorists have proposed that an identity is a theory of self (Berzonsky, 1993; Grotevant, 1987). Berzonsky defines identity as "a conceptual structure composed of postulates, assumptions, and constructs relevant to the self interacting in the world (1993, p.169)."

Extending the conception of identity as a theory of self, Berzonsky (1993) suggests that we view the individual as a self-theorist engaged in a process of theorizing about the self. Taking a constructivist view, he argues that this theorizing is not simply a matter of gathering and summarizing data and testing predictions. Rather, theorizing involves an active process of interpreting one's experiences and generating new ones.

Berzonsky (1993) distinguished three types of self-theorists marked by different styles of theorizing: (a) scientific self-theorists, (b) dogmatic self-theorists, and (c) ad hoc self-theorists.

Scientific self-theorists (informational identity style), tend to be self-reflective, skeptical about self-constructions, and open to self-relevant information. An informational style entails a willingness to investigate multiple solutions to a given problem and to explore several options before committing to any one(Berzonsky,1993). Information-oriented individuals deal with personal decisions and identity concerns by deliberately seeking out, processing, and evaluating self-relevant information.

Dogmatic self-theorists,(normative identity style) in contrasts, conform to "the values and expectations of significant others (including parents). They use self-serving efforts... to defend against potential threats to their self-constructions. Individuals who utilize this protectionist approach to self-theorizing, have been found to endorse authoritarian views, to possess rigid self-construct systems, and to be closed to novel information relevant to hard core values and beliefs (Berzonsky,1992,1993)

Ad hoc Self-theorists (diffuse/avoidance identity style) continually react to situational demands. A poorly organized, fragmented self-theory leads people to procrastinate and avoid dealing with personal conflicts and decisions. If one waits long enough, situational demands and consequences will eventually determine behavioral reactions (Berzonsky,1993).

The three constructs used in this research, relate to different aspects of "self". One of these aspects which comprises the "self" in social interactions and in relation with others, is "self-assertion". An individual who has a clear understanding of oneself and a sense of commitment to ones beliefs and values, is expected to express them more confidently and definitely in social circumstances, especially in situations where the cultural context also considers self-assertion as a positive and valuable phenomenon and encourages self-assertive people. Seen from this view, self-assertion not only has a personal intrapsychic dimension, but also involves a social element as it is manifested in interpersonal interactions.

Another aspect of self, is self efficacy. A new vision of adolescence points to the individual strengths that promote positive development (Damon and Gregory, 2003). It has become clear that individuals play a proactive role in their adaptation rather than simply undergo experiences that act on their personal liabilities (Bandura,2006). In this regard, self-efficacy beliefs are among the knowledge structures that exert a pervasive influence on youths' successful development. Unless young people believe they can produce desired results by their actions, they have little incentive to undertake activities or to persevere in the face of difficulties (Bandura, 1997).

Over the years, findings have attested to the role that multi-faceted self-efficacy beliefs exert in sustaining positive behaviors and preventing maladaptive behaviors over the course of adolescence.

Thus, the present investigation, through studying 3 constructs, will focus on "self" as the main core of personality. If "self" has developed and has enough solidarity or integrity ego-strength then it is, expected that it manifests itself in different aspects of an individual's life including the ways he processes the concepts related to oneself, others, and the environment.

In an investigation on the relationship between identity style and self-assertion, Schwartz et al. (2000) concluded that participants with an informational style of identity, scored the highest and those who resorted to identity diffusion/ avoidance style, scored the lowest on the individual self-assertion scale. In another study (Schwartz et al. 2000) with university students, the mean individual self-assertion score of individuals with the normative style was found to be significantly higher than those with the Identity diffusion style. The results, however, indicated no significant difference between the scores of information-oriented and normative groups. Gordon (1989) and Waterman et al. (2000) also found a significant, positive relationship between personal self-assertion and identity achievement; but no significant difference was observed between foreclosure and moratorium identity statues on self-assertion. Piri and Shahraray (2005) found there is the positive relationship between Informational Identity style and positive assertiveness. There is negative relation between defuse/avoidance identity style and assertiveness and there is no relationship between normative identity style and assertiveness.

In an investigation about the relation between self identity style and self-efficacy. Jakubowski, Dembo, and Myron (2004) in their research among college students found that there is positive relationship between self-efficacy and Informational identity style and negative relationship with defuse/avoidance identity style.

Since the relationship between identity styles and self-assertion and self-efficacy is a very significant, appealing issue and also because it has not been studied in the fairly collective context of India, the researcher have decided to undertake this investigation. Another reason for conducting this study, was to gain a deeper knowledge into the relationship between self-assertion and identity styles and between self-assertion and self-efficacy among university students in India.

Methodology

Participants

From the population of first year male students in pune university, 124 science students who are 18 years old, were selected by randomly Sampeling.

Research Instruments

The present study used the following 3 questionnaires to measure self-assertion, identity styles, and General self-efficacy.

Assertiveness Questionnaire

This 80-item questionnaire has been designed by Towned (1994).There are 80 statements, which participants will respond with "yes" if the statement is like or true of him/her, and "No" if the statement is unlike or untrue of him/her. This questionnaire includes 4 categories of self- assertion behaviors; namely passive, manipulative, aggressive and assertive. The reliability of this questionnaire is .82 (Towned, 1994) and this research by Alpha coefficient found .84.

Scores 14-20, suggest that this is how participants regularly think and feel about theirselves and others. Scores 7-13, suggest that this is how participants frequently think and feel about theirselves and others. Scores 0-6, suggest that this is how they rarely think and feel about theirselves and others.

Identity style Inventory (ISI-G6)

This 40-item Inventory (Berzonsky,1997) measures 3 identity styles, namely Informational Diffuse/Avoidance, and Normative styles of identity and the degree of individuals' commitment. 11 items assesses the Informational style, 9 items the normative style, and 10 items taps the diffuse/avoidant style, and 10 items measure commitment scale. Items are responded to on 5-point Likert-type scales with"completely agree (5)","some how agree (4)", "I'm not sure (3)","some how disagree (2)", and"completely disagree (1)". Categorical measures of Style are obtained by standardizing the three Style Scores and using the style with the highest standard score (Berzonsky,1997; White, Wampler and Winn,1998). Coefficient alphas are as follows, For the Information scale .59, diffuse/avoidant scale .78, and normative scale .64 (Berzonsky, 1992, 1997; White, Wampler and Winn, 1998).

Berzonsky (2000) reported the Cronbach alpha coefficients of informational, normative, and diffused/ avoidant style and commitment scale to be .71, .64, .75, and .78, respectively. Using the same method, in this investigation estimated reliability was .58, .69, .51, for informational, diffused/avoidant, normative identity styles.

General Self-efficacy Scale

This 10-item scale is designed by Matthias Jerusalem and Ralf Schwarzer(1992). Responses are made on a 4-point scale. Sum up the responses to all 10 items to yield the final composite score with a range from 10 to 40. In samples from 23 nations, Cronbach's alphas ranged from .76 to .90, with the majority in the high .80s. The scale is unidimensional in this research by same method, the reliability is .79.

Procedure

Before administering the measures, participants were informed about the objectives of the research and told that their participation is voluntary. Following their consent, the assertion Inventory(AI), the Identity Style questionnaire, and the General Self-efficacy Scale was completed individually.

Results

In this research for investigating the relationship between self-assertiveness and self-identity styles the pearson cofficient used. Table 1 and 2 represent statistical indexes, calculated by the SPSS software. There was no defuse identity style among participants.

TABLE - 1

Estimated Indexes of the Significance Test of the Observed Correlation between Informational Identity Style and Assertion Scales

Indexes Assertion Scale	*Pearson Coefficient*	*N*	*D.F.*	*estimated tr.*	*α*
Manipulative behavior	.106	32	30	0.60	—
Passive behavior	.186	32	30	1.05	0.05
Assertion behavior	.301	32	30	1.73	0.01
Aggressive behavior	-.307	32	30	-1.42	—

As indicated in table1.informational style has relation amount 0.30 with aseertion behavior at the 0.99 confidence interval and 0.18 with passive behavior at the .95 confidence interval. It does not have any relation with munipulative and aggressive behavior. The reasons which created these results will be discussed in discussion part. Table 2 represents statistical indexes which related to the relation between normative identity style and assertion scales.

TABLE - 2

Estimated Indexes of the Significance Test of the Observed Correlation between Normative Identity Style and Assertion Scales.

Indexes Assertion Scale	*Pearson Coefficient*	*N*	*D.F.*	*estimated tr.*	*α*
Assertion behavior	.040	92	90	0.40	—
Passive behavior	.354	92	90	3.50	0.01
Manipulative behavior	.160	92	90	1.53	—
Aggressive behavior	-.026	92	90	- 0.189	—

As indicated in table 2 the normative identity style has the relation amount 0.35 with passive behavior at the .99 confidence interval. For investigating the relationship between identity styles and self-efficacy in this research again the pearson coefficient estimated which showed in Table 3.

TABLE - 3
Estimated Indexes of the Significance Test of the Observed Correlation between Self-Identity Styles and Self-efficacy Scale.

Indexes Identity Styles	*Pearson Coefficient*	*N*	*D.F.*	*estimated tr.*	*α*
Informational	0.30	32	30	1.74	0.01
Normative	0.24	92	90	2.34	0.005

Discussion

As reported in Table 1, Findings revealed a positive correlation between informational identity style, (32 participants) and assertion behavior. They use assertion behavior regularly. These findings are consistent with the results by Schwartz et al. (2000), Gordon (1989), Waterman et al. (2000), and Waterman and Manion (2000). Townend (1994) suggests that assertion most of all is based on the development of self-confidence.

Informational individuals are concerned about the autonomy of themselves and others in their interpersonal interactions and put an equal value in the beliefs, ideas, thoughts and feelings of themselves and others (Riss and Graham, 1991). In sum, Informational individuals, given their particular characteristics and cognitive-behavioral components have a higher motivation and skill for being assertive.

This finding indicates that individuals with informational identity style also tend to behave passively. This finding is opposite of another researches.

It seems that self- assertion depends not only on an individual's personality aspects, but also on the cultural values of the community and the extent to which self-assertion is encouraged or discouraged by the society. For example, in the collective culture of china, where the "self" is defined only in relation with others, modesty, tolerance and attempt to establish and maintain a friendly relation with others might be preferred and valued more than self-assertion (Hargie, 1997). In such an interdependent, community-based culture,"self" harmoniously interacts with others, is flexible and tolerant, assumes responsibility for others' expectations, feelings, and preferences and is anxious to adjust oneself to others (Markus and Kitayama, 1991). The Individualist cultures (like North America), on the other hand, believe that every individual must be independent, and that one can enter the society and establish social relations only based on ones' own needs and through a bilateral agreement with others (Markus and Kitayama, 1991; 1994; Schweder et al., 1997). "Self" in this kind of culture, is stable, independent, is influenced by ones' personal characteristics, goals and preferences, and is honest, explicit self-controlled, self-promotive, and assertive (www.edu.css 2004).

As indicated there is positive relation between normative identity style and passive behavior.

Given that individuals with the normative identity style tend to obey authorities and are usually closed to new information (Berzonsky and Ferrari, 1996), and especially information that They might have explored and assessed individually, there is a possibility that They might have been committed to parents who have mostly used or reinforced the passive behavior and therefore created a situation for their boys to emulate.

This finding is consistent with the findings of Gordon (1989), Waterman and Manion (1994), and Waterman et al. (2000). Normatives, compared to the other two groups, have a higher level of conformity to and dependence on authorities; they are lower in independence and self-confidence and are less willing to think about themselves (Berzonsky,1992). Since they seek confirmation by others and consider other peoples' right to be more important than their own, normatives think they would lose respect if they behave assertively. So in most cases they might show self-assertion lest they would lose the relationship. This might be more probable in collective contexts such as India.

Findings also shows that the informational identity style has stronger relationship with self-efficacy (0.30) rather than the normative identity style which had 0.24. Jakubowski, Dembo, and Myron (2004) in their research among college students found that there is positive relationship between self-efficacy and Informational identity style. Informational individuals almost rarely seek confirmation by others and are often confident about their own judgements. Compared to the other two groups, they have a higher degree of flexibility and tolerance in novel situations. They are so away from their abilities rather than the other kinds of identity styles.

As an original research in India this study contains a number of limitations that needs to be attended to in future studies. The sample was Comprised exclusively of university male students in Pune. Therefore, female student, male and female Students from different ages, and participants from other regions in the country were not studied. To increase external validity, future studies should include other samples. The use of self-report methodology especially in areas Concerned with Self is an obvious limitation. Better forms of operationalizing identity, Self-assertiveness as well as self efficacy would allow for more reliable knowledge withinthis important area of inquiry in India.

REFERENCES

Alberti, R. and Emmons, M. L. (1982). Your perfect right: A guide to assertive behavior (4th.ed) san luis Obispo. Impact publishers .

Bandura, A. (1986). *Social foundations of thought and action: a social cognitive theory*. Englewood Cliffs, NJ: Prentice Hall.

Bandura, A. (2006). Adolescent development from an agentic perspective. In F. Pajares and T. Urdan (Eds.), Self-efficacy beliefs of adolescents (Vol. 5, pp. 1–43). Greenwich, CT: Information Age Publishing.

Bandura, A. (1997). *Self-efficacy: The exercise of control.* New York: Freeman.

Bandura, A. (2006). Adolescent development from an agentic perspective. In F. Pajares and T. Urdan (Eds.), Self-efficacy beliefs of adolescents (Vol. 5, pp. 1–43). *Greenwich, CT: Information Age Publishing.*

Berzonsky, M .D.(1993).A constructive view of identity development:People as postpositivist self-theorists.In J.Kroger(Ed.),Discussions on ego identity (pp.169-203).Hillsdale,NJ:Erlbaum.

Berzonsky, M.D and Ferrari,J.R. (1996). Identity orientation and decisional strategies . Journal of Personality and Individual Differences. 20, 597-606.

Berzonsky , M. D.(1992). Identity styles and coping strategies. Journal of Personality .60(4), 771-788.

Berzonsky, M. D .(1997).Identity development, control theory, and self- regulation:An individual differences perspective.Journal of Adolescent Research, 12, 347-353.

Berzonsky, M.D. (2000). Literature review(Personal communication with Berzonsky).

Bower, S. A and Bower, . H .(1978). *Asserting Yourself (A practical guide for positive change). Addison- Wesleg Publishing Compang Inc*

Bower, Sharon Anthonyand Bower, Gordon.H .(1976).*Asserting your self (a practical guide for positive change*). Addison- wesleg Publishing Compang Inc.

Cairns, R. B., and Cairns, B. D. (1994). *Lifelines and risks: Pathways of youth in our time.* New York: Cambridge University Press

Chan ,W ,D. (1993).*Components of Assertiveness: Their relationships with assertive rights and depressed mood among Chinese college students in Hongkong. Behavior Research andThrapy. 31(5), 529- 538.*

Compas, B. E., Hinden, B. R., and Gerhardt, C. A. (1995). Adolescent development: Pathways and processes of risk and resilience. *Annual Review of Psychology, 46, 265–293.*

Cote, J. E. and Levin, C. (1988). A critical examination of the ego identity status paradigm.Developmental Review, 8, 147-184.

Cultural Dimensions. (2004). www.css.edu.

Damon, W., and Gregory, A. (2003). *Bringing in a new era in the field of youth development*. In R. M. Lerner and P. L.

Erikson, E .H.(1968).Identity: Youth and Crisis.New York:Norton.

Folkman, S. and Lazarus, R. S. (1988). The relationship between coping and emotion: Implications for theory and research. Social and Medicine, 26 , 309-317.

Galassi M.D and Galassi J.P. (1978). Assertion: A critical review Psychotherapy: Theory Research and Practice, 15, 16.29.

Grotevant, H. D. (1987).Toward a process model of identity formation.Journal of Adolescent Research, 2, 203-222.

Gordon, L.L. (1989). Identity development and personal expressiveness.Unpublished MA Thesis. University of Arizona.

Hargie,W. O. (1997). The Handbook of Communication Skills (2nd ed.) NewYork: Routledge.

Jakubowski, T. G.and Dembo, M. H.(2004). The Relationship of Self-Efficacy, Identity Style, and Stage of Change with Academic Self-Regulation *Journal of College Reading and Learning, v35 n1 p7-24.*

Lerner, R. M., and Steinberg, L. (2004). *The scientific study of adolescent development. Past, present, and future*. In R.

Lazarus, A.A. (1973). On assertive beharior: A brief note. Behavior Therapy ,4. 697 -699

Longe, A.J and Jakubowski. P. (1987). The assertive option : Your Right and Responsibilities. Champeign ,Illinois: Research Press.

Marcia, J. E. (1966).Development and validation of ego identity status. Journal of Personality and Social Psychology ,3, 551-558.

Markus, H. R and Kitayama, S. H. (1991). Culture and the Self: Implication for Cognition, Emotion and Motivation.Psychological Review. 98 (2). 224-253.

Muris, P. (2001).*Relationships between self-efficacy and symptoms of anxiety disorders and depression in a normal adolescent sample*. Elsevi er Science Ltd.

Muris, P. (2001).Relationships between self-efficacy and symptoms of anxiety disorders and depression in a normal adolescent sample. *Elsevi er Science Ltd.*

Piri, L and Shahraray, M.(2005).*Relationship between Ego Identity Styles, Self-assertiveness and Coping Styles*. Unpublished master's thesis, Teacher Training University.

Persona, S and Persona, L. M. (1993). Relationships among Minuchins structural family model, identity , achievement and coping styie. Journal of Counseling Psychology. 40, (4), 479-489.

Riss, S and Graham, R.S. (1991). Assertion Training: How to be who you really are? Printed in Great Britain by Mackays of Chatham PLC.

Rodriquez, G. (2001). Significant variables associated with assertiveness among Hispanic college women. Journal of Instructional Psychology. 1-6.

Renk, K. and Creasey , G . (2003). The relationship of gender, gender identity , and coping strategies in late adolescents. Journal of Adolescence 26, 159- 1680.

Sheridan, C.L and Radmacher, S. A. (1992). Health Psychology :Challenging the Biomedical Model. New york: John Wiley and sons,Inc.

Schwartz , S; Mullis, R. L ; Waterman, A andDunham, R .M .(2000). Ego identity status, identity style, and personal expressiveness: An Empirical investigation of three convergent constructs. Journal of Adolescent Research. 15(4), 504-521.

Soenens, B; Duriez , B and Goossens, L. (2003). Social- psychological profiles of identity styles : Attitudinal and social - cognitive correlates in late Adolescence. (in print)

Shweder, R; Goodnow, J; Hatano, G, Levine, R; Markus , H and Miller, P. (1997). The cultural psychology of development : One mind , many mentalities; Damon, Wand Lerner, R. M. Handbook of Child Psychology . (fifth edition). Volume 1. Theoretical Models of Human Development.

Townend, Anni. (1994). Developing assertiveness .(2ed). London : Routledge.

White, J. M; Wampler,R andWinn,K.I .(1998).The identity style inventory: A revision with a sixth- grade reading level (ISI_ 6G). Journal of Adolescent Research,13(2),pp.223-245.

Waterman ,A .S; Lopez ,L .M;Gruenfeld, K .E and Jessee,C .L.(2000). The relationship of personal expressiveness to intrinsic motivation, purpose in life, identity achievement,and principled morality. Manuscript in preparation, The college of New Jersey Ewing.

Waterman, A .S and Mannion ,K .(1994).On the relationship of optimal experience to identity formation, psychosocial identity, and self- actualization. Paper presented at the biennial meeting of the International Society for the Study of Behavioral Development. Amsterdam.

6

THE MENTAL HEALTH PROBLEMS IN CHILDREN

Challenges of 21st Century

An Alternative model of emergence of mental health problems in children

Mili Jaswal and Tripathi S. K.

Much of the research and thinking in the area of childhood temperament has been guided by the structural and measurement model; recently, researchers have called into question this structural conception and have explored the factor structure of the instruments. A review of the literature indicates that there are few studies at any one age level, and that much of the research is limited by small samples. The results of a large sample factor analysis of parent and teacher ratings of preschool children are reported. Recent ecological studies, focused on the impact of school setting (Barker and Gump,1964). The findings showed that pupils attending small as opposed to large high schools received and enhanced extracurricular experience. A greater percentage of them feat a responsibility to become involved in activities, and held positions of leadership and responsibility. In small schools, there were fewer outsiders that is pupils on the fringe who did not participate at all. The ecosystem refers to social settings that do not actually contain children; but, that nevertheless, affect their experience in immediate settings. In accordance with the findings of recent literatures; ***an alternative model for emergence of mental health problems in children*** *has been conceived as most appropriate for parent education, and a solution seemed most appropriate for teacher's training are discussed.*

Mental Health is the embodiment of social, emotional and spiritual well-being. Mental health provides individuals with the vitality necessary for active living, to achieve goals and to interact with one another in ways that are respectful and just. Internationally, there is growing awareness of the interrelationship between our social environments; the care and nurturing we receive when young; our interactions with others and sense of inclusion and our mental health and emotional well-being. Issues such as housing, town planning, education, employment and transport all have a role to play in determining the mental health of the population. Mental illness results from complex causal interactions and is influenced by a number of risk and protective factors. Low self-esteem, lack of control over work and home life, insecurity and continuing uncertainty all contribute to long-term stress and may result in mental health problems. The unemployed and socially isolated people have higher prevalence of mental health disorders than do people who are employed and socially connected. Experiences in childhood and negotiation of life changes have profound effects on mental health across the life span. These effects can be minimized within a strong and supportive community environment (Hagel, 2004).

Mental health is a national health priority area. Research indicates that close to 20% of Indians were affected by a mental health problem within a given twelve months period, with more than 25% of young adults (18 to 24)suffering from at least one mental disorder over this period (including co-morbidity with substance misuse). The prevalence of mental health problems is similar for children and young people ranging from 14% to 20% in any given year (*Food and Behaviour Research*). The institutional and non-institutional costs of mental disorders are in themselves overwhelming, however, other costs include impacts on families and communities; the need for welfare responses, coronial work (in the case of suicides), absenteeism from work, loss of earnings, legal costs and diminished quality of life.

Mental Health in terms of emotional and social well-being is a key public health issue which requires comprehensive, inter sectoral action. Mental Health problems can predispose people to unemployment, social isolation and discrimination. Social isolation and discrimination also contribute to mental health problems. Improving the social environment in schools, home, and developing strong and supportive networks across the life course can impact positively on mental health strengthening both community and individual resilience builds capacity to positively manage periods of transition throughout life given the links between mental health and other aspects of health, partnership approaches with other health and related services are required in order to improve population mental health.

The mental health of the Indian population is a resource for the attainment of some of the Govt.'s strategic policy objectives, such as to put INDIA back on the path to long-term prosperity, to sustain India's commitment to solidarity and social justice, and to bring tangible practical benefits to the quality of life for Indian children (Hagel, 2004). However, the mental health of the Indian population can be considerably improved: Mental ill health affects every fourth citizen and can lead to suicide, a cause of too many deaths; Mental ill health causes significant losses and burdens to the economic, social, educational as well as criminal and justice systems; stigmatization, discrimination and non-respect for the human rights and the dignity of mentally ill and disabled people still exist, challenging core European values. Improvement is possible. Many initiatives have already been taken. Further development and consolidation of the existing actions is required.

There is no health without mental health. For *citizens*, mental health is a resource which enables them to realize their intellectual and emotional potential and to find and fulfill their roles in social, school and working life. For *societies*, good mental health of citizens contributes to prosperity, solidarity and social justice. In contrast, mental ill health imposes manifold costs, losses and burdens on citizens and societal systems.

Up until relatively recently it seemed that the different theoretical approaches to understanding the origin of children's mental health problems existed in isolation from each other. When brought together they were more likely to lead to competitive discussion and rivalry than thoughtful reflection and critical analysis. Thankfully, the polarized nature versus nurture debate is largely in the past and the interrelationships between those factors that are associated with child developmental outcomes are now widely acknowledged to be complex. We have moved far away from assuming that factors associated with risk are necessarily the direct cause of problems. Likewise we no longer consider risk factors alone without also taking into account factors that promote resilience in children and young people. Simplistic statements that promote single causes of mental health problems in children, whether it be the role of diet, poverty, genes or other relevant associated factors, are clearly misleading. This record of the presentations and discussion at the seminar hosted by Young Minds and the Institute for Public Policy Research brings together a range of different perspectives and research findings that illustrate the complexity of the issues that need to be disentangled. However, what emerges are not just the differences in understanding but also the commonalities. It is the latter that demonstrates the progress that has been made in integrating the knowledge now available, but there is still much more to learn.

As we seek answers, more questions emerge. I hope that this excellent attempt to achieve a synthesis of the research evidence will be the model for the future.

Mental Health, Mental Ill Health and Its Determinants

The WHO describes **mental health** as: "a state of well-being in which the individual realizes his or her abilities, can cope with the normal stresses of life, can work productively and fruitfully, and is able to make a contribution to his or her community" (*Food and Behaviour Research*).

Mental ill health includes mental health problems and strain, impaired functioning associated with distress, symptoms, and diagnosable mental disorders, such as schizophrenia and depression. Mental condition of people is determined by a **multiplicity of factors** including biological (e.g., genetics, gender), individual (e.g., personal experiences), family and social (e.g., social support) and economic and environmental (e.g., social status and living conditions).

The important emotional interchanges in the family are not solely of gratifyingly positive feelings. Anger, jealousy and resentment can be a part also, and these also enrich the total experience if the more mutually gratifying feelings are predominant. Children are frequently facile in verbalizing their hostile responses while they are inarticulate in expressing the more deeply felt feelings of affection. Some adults are like that too.

The word family has implications over and above a description of its numerical composition. It is a living form rather than a filing cabinet. As such, because of the emotional gratification that lies in the individual's relationship to it, its characteristics are a composite of all those of its contributing members, but with a unique pattern resulting from a fusion of all. When it or any member of it is threatened from outside, it arouses loyalty and protectiveness that erases negative feelings within the group. The family is defended against an outside enemy, irrespective of the internal turmoil that exists. Members of a family respond as parts of total body. An individual may consider his physical form undesirable, or one essential part of it particularly unattractive, yet he will protect every part of his body from attack by others regardless of his own dislike for a part of it and his own attempts to modify or hide it. Pain or pleasure is experienced by the total physical body even though the pain or pleasure is localized in only a part of the body. Equally so, the family responds totally to the experiences of one part.

Even when, with justification, the individual rejects his family, if his earlier experiences had some meaningfulness to him, this rejection is not without emotional repercussions. These repercussions are often either in the area of shame or guilt. Shame is experienced when a member of the family behaves contrary to the individual's concept of propriety or good taste. Guilt is experienced if an individual behaves contrary to family standards, attacks members of the family or violates social morals. He wonders what "the family will say". The individual feels guilty as the result of the meaning his behaviour will have to the family. He fears he will lose the love of the family group. Behaviour of another member will also arouse his guilt. He will strive to make up for the act of one who violated some family standard, as if the entire family shared the crime and would be punished for it.

It is difficult to know when the full meaning of the family develops. Its development is probably insidious and would be expected to be rather nebulous in outline until the more primary relationships with the individual members composing the family have reached a point of some stability and predictableness. As indication of this a child whose relationship with his mother has never been adequately stabilized, will tend to continue with that relationship rather than find value in the give-and-take of a family group. The significance of the family can be traced throughout the psychological development of the individual.

As the small child becomes aware of the interest and protectiveness of the other members of the family in addition to the mother he finds those other members offer him security as well. The family becomes a depersonalized mother. This meaning of family usually continues through life. A common phrase gives expression to the emotional significance of this concept: "he returned to the bosom of his family."

The family plays an important role for the child as he struggles to achieve some equilibrium between (and some safety in spite of) his need both to love and to express his hostilely motivated impulses. It is important to recognize the validity and the strengthening effect of the hostile responses occurring in the emotional interchanges in the family. Such interchanges give the individual an opportunity to be a total person and in so being to learn to so constructively. It is inevitable that an individual who has not repressed a fairly extensive part of himself will feel resentment, jealousy, anger and destructive impulses as long as he is a part of the world. Those emotions expressed in unmodified form would militate against any really successful adaptation, not only to the world outside of himself , but also to his own internal being. These emotions, which in their unmitigated form would have eventually to be repressed, can be gradually redirected as a result of childhood learning experiences into acceptable and often more dynamically productive outlets. This is most facilely achieved in an emotional atmosphere in which the individual has acceptance as a person even though his act may not be acceptable.

It is in the family that the child can most readily learn to tolerate and balance these ambivalent feelings. In no other interpersonal relationship is hostility so sharply weighted against the heavier element of love. In no other interpersonal relationship is the ambivalent response of the other person so weighted in favor of affection. In few situations, further, are the ambivalent feelings towards another so tangibly colored by the value of the total of which each individual is a part. Not only does the child seek to reestablish and solidify his relationship with the individual toward whom his ambivalent feelings are directed but he wishes to preserve his place in the intimate group. This is clearly indicated in certain domestic crises. A child is angry at his mother and directs the anger towards every near. His mother recognizing herself as the real target withdraws his from the family circle to attempt to establish peace between the child and herself. Once her mission is completed the child frequently wants not to remain alone with her but return to the family group. The mother unconsciously recognizes this when she suggests that maybe he would like to go downstairs again. This readiness to return to the group is not only to share activities. Often the other members maybe quietly pursuing different and solo activities. The child appears to spread the newly achieved equilibrium to his relationship to the group, not only to the meaningful person who disrupted it.

The association between variables in the family context and the risk for emotional/behavioral problems in children in a Family Health Progragmme, using A cross-sectional design study ,100 children aged 6 to 12 years old and their families, especially their biological mothers (82%)were studied. Emotional/behavioral problems of the child, in levels considered as at risk for the development of disorders, were identified by means of the Strengths and Difficulties Questionnaire. Regarding conditions in the family context, the following variables were evaluated: socio-economic level, adverse events, maternal stress, maternal depressive symptoms, organization, and structure of family environment. Data analysis was performed through unvaried and multivariate logistic regression. Maternal stress was associated with general mental health problems in the child (OR=2.2), while a daily routine with an organized timetable and greater range of activities to fill up their free time were associated with the absence of these problems (1/OR 1.3 and 1.9, respectively). Maternal stress was also a risk factor for anxiety/depression symptoms (OR=1.6). Regarding hyperactivity, financial instability was a risk factor (OR=2.1), and all indicators of environmental stability were protective variables (1/OR between 1.2 and 1.6). Information about family context indicators associated with mental health problems in schoolchildren may subsidize actions of the Family Health Program teams for the child and his/her family. A child also needs the assurance that adults will carry part of the responsibility for his behavior. Given freedom beyond his ability to govern himself, a child can be very frightened. He may show this insecurity by impulse, reckless behavior that would seem to indicate fearlessness but that actually is a denial of the fear. He may, on the other hand, disclose his insecurity by complete inhibition of his own actions .In each instance his ego is not working with its full potential. A brilliant boy very clearly expressed his reaction to a totally permissive environment. He was severely inhibited, as if he feared always that any spontaneous act on his part would prove catastrophic. His parents were convinced member of the cult of unlimited self-expression for the children, without any adult direction. The child's therapist, after many unproductive hours with the child, finally commented with non-professional exasperation that the boys behavior did not make sense. He could do anything he wanted to, and yet he never let himself do anything. "Can't you see why?" he immediately replied. "Never have my parents said this is the right way ,that is the wrong way ,this is safe, that is dangerous .I haven't lived long enough to know what is right and what is wrong, what is safe and what is dangerous .I'm afraid of what I might do." An environment that defined wise limits for the child brought about a rapid liberation from his self-imposed imprisonment.

Children do not have the living experience to know what is dangerous and what is safe. Furthermore, they may have many contradictory impulses that they can't reconcile. They need guidance in finding safe satisfactions for internal urges and safe responses to external stimulations. Only after long experience can they even begun to direct their own behavior wisely. If expected to do so too early, they may be in real danger, and may fear other dangers that actually do not exist. A child needs freedom in order to mature healthily. To avoid the dangers of license, he needs that freedom within limits that can be defined only by the sophistication and judgment of adults.

This concept of a framework for children, realistically applied, results in what appears to be a contradiction. As the child develops a capacity to handle his own impulses not only is he given more freedom but greater demands are placed on him by those around him. Consider the problem of the child who has strong aggressive impulses that he as yet does not know how to handle. At the same time he has poor table manners. Inability to handle aggressive impulses in a socially and personally constructive way can have serious repercussions. Table manners are of secondary importance to this more primary conflict. If the child is frightened by his own impulses, he needs the assurance of wise restrictions upon their expression. He may also need guidance in order to channel his aggression constructively. Provided with such a framework, he gains confidence and suitable patterns for expressing his aggressiveness within it. During this period ideally the question of table manners is ignored. Every effort is concentrated on helping him feel more comfortable with his aggressive drives. Prohibitions and permissions are defined and controlled by someone outside of himself. Finally he develops ways of expressing his aggressiveness satisfactory both to himself and to his social world. No longer is he dependent upon the restrictions imposed by others; he has mastered those restrictions himself. At this point he is ready for the struggle to attain table manners.

There are certain fundamental urges that a child first learns to handle. As he struggles to find a pattern for them, adult-imposed limits serve as a guide. When more basic urges are mastered, the child can tackle the finer points of social living. Through the flexibility of the framework established by the adults, the more primitive fundamental urges are first directed into constructive outlets; then and only then, are the secondary aspects of social living brought into the total growth picture. This does not mean, to take table manners as an example, that the child should not be encouraged to use a knife and fork until he has directed his aggressive impulses into adult channels. It means rather that such secondary adjustments are most wisely taught during periods when the child's primary adaptive patterns are adequate to deal with the demands reality places upon him.

As the child becomes familiar with his external world, his adaptation to it will be more adequate if he finds suitable ways of expressing impulses, which, in undirected form, are contradictory or unacceptable. To the extent that he can find gratifying channels of expression for his impulse, the child will be psychologically healthier. He will be free of anxiety, will have more emotional energy. He will develop more completely his total psychological potential if he does not have to hold in check part of it because in its unmodified form it is destructive rather than constructive.

The majority of cases of adult psychiatric problem, symptoms were first identified between the ages of 11-15.12 Substance use in adults is typically preceded by anti-social behaviour, and personality disorder by conduct disorder, for example.12 Violent behaviour peaks between the ages of 17 and 18.13 14 Half of juvenile offenders are active by the age of 12/13.14 Violent behaviour is known to be linked to impulsivity and low IQ, behaviour and conduct disorders, poor parental supervision and abuse and poor performance in school.13 14

The following conclusions can be drawn after considering the patterns of violence in different age groups: [15]

- There is continuity in problem behaviour from childhood to adolescence, especially physical aggression.
- Chronic physical aggression during elementary school increases the risk of violence persisting.
- Physical aggression peaks around the second year of life but then will show different developmental trajectories.
- Violence is unlearned, not learned. Early violence is common and most children become gradually less violent from the time they start school, although indirect aggression increases.

* *Social influences seem to compromise the processes that help to contain violent behaviour. It suggests the quality of early relationship experiences is important.*

This was further indicated by one study that compared

the reactions of teenage mothers to simple images of contrasting affective states with a control group of mothers.[16]

- The teenage mothers selected were considered rejecting, suffered from depression and had low IQ. They were far less sensitive to the different emotions shown in the pictures, even when these were colour-coded in advance; and concurrent brain scans indicated significantly fewer areas of the brain actively involved in the differentiation process than in the control group – a pattern that would have been established during childhood.

The socialization of natural aggression is largely attachment based.

Rejecting mothers are often angry, so their children observe anger as a predominant emotion. Some infants appear fearless, which could be linked to rejection or anger. These children won't seek maternal or adult contact for safety. One study of guilt in four and a half year-olds showed those who'd been fearless infants demonstrated no guilt.[17]

'Mentalisation' would seem to be another key explanatory factor relating to mental health. This is a unique human capacity that enables us to experience the subjective experience of our fellow humans. We interpret our own behaviour in terms of the mental states of others.

Violence has a human price because it directly interferes with mentalisation. Violence is adaptive. Society has created taboos around violence because of its incompatibility with experiencing subjective state. Violent individuals often have an impaired or inhibited capacity for mentalisation: gun use requires less inhibition than knife use; violence is easier when there is anonymity rather than proximity. Children who are maltreated feel anonymous; they feel they cannot be seen or recognized.

it is clear that what is needed is a significant research programme focusing on child and adolescent mental health and he hoped that we can take advantage of some of the opportunities that are becoming available. The points on which we need agreement either openly or implicitly included:

- Individual differences are important: people react differently to similar stimuli that can be social, biochemical or environmental. Some of these individual differences may be genetically influenced.
- Nature versus nurture is a false dichotomy – too many factors intervene to alter possible or probable causal pathways. Our genes merely determine predispositions, not precise outcomes.
- We need to take far more seriously the associative connections that undoubtedly exist between mind and body, which seem to be stronger than many supposed.
- What we eat (nutrition) and our perceptions and reactions to stress (cortisol and its aftermath) undoubtedly affect the biochemistry of our brains and bodies in fundamental ways. This is likely to affect behaviour patterns and control mechanisms (impulsivity).
- The causes of mental health problems in adults are many and complex and do not lend themselves to simple solutions and interventions. Nonetheless, clearer patterns within causal pathways are emerging from research and the search for interrelated, effective interventions should continue.
- When identifying solutions, it is vital to differentiate between the predicament/environment of a particular individual and that of the group (age, area, socio-economic status, ethnicity).
- The origins of mental health issues in adults will invariably lie in past experiences.
- Socio-economic status can have a profound impact on individual behaviour, for a range of different reasons, and these must be assessed carefully.
- Mental health problems and disorders can be viewed as the outcome of impaired, delayed or otherwise inhibited normal healthy development; as a rational yet often dysfunctional reaction to a difficult or challenging

context; and as a dysfunctional, more extreme manifestation of an otherwise normal and functional state of mind.

Exploring Synthesis

What follows is an attempt to explore in greater depth the overlap between different professional perspectives (not necessarily covered in the presentations) and the potential for further agreement in understanding the possible causes of mental disorders.

Time Trends and Vulnerability to Mental Health Problems

In the light of the evident continuum of behaviour mentioned by a number of speakers, we might consider adolescence less as a discrete explosion and more as a period during which earlier difficulties that may have been either hidden or manageable hitherto become exposed or re-exposed. If adolescence is turbulent largely because of the identity crisis elicited by the physical, neurobiological and hormonal changes, one can suppose that a robust pre-adolescent sense of self will provide some protection. The pre-teen years (8-12 years) are increasingly understood to be a crucial time for the crystallization of identity that, from about the age of eight, encompasses gender, social acceptability and competence. 18 Children take their view of themselves, informed by their treatment within the family, and test this on the world outside (friends, peers and teachers). Their stronger bodies and more reflective and capable minds provide the chance to improve their range of skills and competence. But if they have no mother or father on whom to model themselves, if their self-image at the start of this period is negative or is undermined during this important stage, if they have few opportunities to develop interests and skills that fuel pride or to practice autonomy, or if they have poor relationship and attachment experiences, then their ability either to do well in school or to form good friendships can be compromised, with potentially devastating consequences. Even those who have no special problems face more intense academic, social and commercial pressures that can shake self-belief.

Resilience and Risk Factors – A Critical Assessment

Resilience is an important theoretical concept as it encompasses the complexity of causal factors. It acknowledges, for example, the influence of both social and environmental factors and individual differences and identifies what helps individuals to cope and what increases the risk that they will not. It also accepts that a particular, perhaps unexpected, event, when added to other earlier or concurrent difficulties apparently coped with, can trigger a behavioural or emotional crisis, while as an isolated event it may not have done so. Resilience arises out of a belief in one's own sense of agency, the ability to deal with change and a repertoire of social problem solving. Having a sense of coherent narrative of personal history that makes sense of the world are both necessary for the formation of a sound identity. The resilience framework does not, however, address causation in depth. This raises a danger that the associated protective and risk factors are given undue prominence in policy, with the more telling underlying causal factors or relationships, contextual influences and implications insufficiently appreciated. This has been alluded to this in his comments on both poverty (as a distal or proximal factor) and education. Personal characteristics that protect individuals (secure attachment, average to high intelligence, good communication, planning and problem-solving skills, humor, reflective capacity, religious faith and easy temperament) are largely inter-related.

A secure attachment will encourage easy communication, reflection and, because the future (based on past experience) feels safe, the inclination to think ahead, sequence actions, plan and develop a 'can-do' approach to anticipated problems. If a child is not securely attached, he is more likely to feel that his very sense of self is under threat. Living in and for the moment, he will have little room for reflection, and consequently less space to feel concern for others (which is crucially important for the development of a rounded and whole personality). Risk factors include features such as poverty, low IQ, poor educational achievement, harsh discipline, parental conflict and a poor environment. Poverty is likely to be problematic not in itself, but because the stresses it creates can lead to poor parenting. It might, however, also be possible that where parents as individuals have deep relationship difficulties, poor capacity for reflection and empathy, volatile reactions to perceived threat and profound self-doubt, this contributes to poor educational outcomes, intermittent work patterns and consequential inadequate income flow. Simply increasing family income, without addressing individual and family experiences, relationships and interactions (e.g. family violence or serial partnering) that can trigger disengagement and poverty, may not reduce the social, health and educational problems that are typically associated with low income.

In the context of mental health, it is interesting to note that protective factors help to deliver feelings of security, significance and connection, whereas risk factors tend to contribute towards the opposite: feelings of insecurity, insignificance and isolation. Such feelings can lead young people to form negative views of themselves, and it is these beliefs which underlie much mental distress.

During the last four decades the subject of growth and development of children has received serious attention of academicians, policy makers and practitioners. Scholars of different disciplines i.e. psychology, psychiatry, home science, pediatrics, education, social work and sociology have placed the child at focal point of their researches. These researches have aimed at understanding scientifically and systematically the determinants and detrimental factors, in the developmental processes of the child. In early "70s" (1974) with the promulgation of a national policy on children, India emerged as a leading national amongst developing countries.

Subsequently, in the year 1975, Government introduced the integrated child development scheme, which was aimed at providing services for the total care and development of the children and women. The cause of children got further impetus with the United Nations assembly declaring 1979 as an international year of the child (IYC). Thereafter, policy makers, subject matter experts on child development and others continued to examine the state of knowledge in the field, so as to decide the priorities and make efforts more effective and concentrated in order to ensure optimistic development of the children.

A critical appraisal of the state of art of children in our country leads us to believe that any programme of child development must take into account the health and nutritional area because of high rate of IMR and malnutrition. As matter of fact there is a reason to believe that in the end malnutrition per se will emerge as only one of the several factors inherent in the "culture" which interacts with other factors in causing the IMR, health problems and other developmental lags like mental retardation.

Since the macro environmental variables do not explain clearly the occurrence of severe malnutrition; therefore, one has to analyze the environment of malnourished children as the ultimate environment of a child in his early childhood stage is his family, because his growth and development strictly depends upon the degree of his competents in meeting his bio-psychological needs within the family. As matter of fact, the growth development of child is product of organism - environment interaction. The sensory organs which are required for deriving experiences from environment (family features e.g. family affective dynamics, quality of parenting and psycho-somatic health status of the mothers), become sharpened and more efficacious in the developmental course of active interplay with environment in producing proper development. Since the larger part of sensory input come from environment, it can be easily assumed that growth and development of a child should be shaped by the characteristics of environment in which the developing organism is placed and to which it is exposed.

Research studies carried out to investigate the micro level factors responsible for malnutrition focused on the quality of child care and mother as the principal stimulating agent for a young child (Cravioto and Delicardie 1976). Apart from that, in other study by Cadwell (1967) above 8 areas of home environment *i.e.*

1. frequency and stability of adult contact
2. vocal stimulation
3. need gratification
4. emotional climate
5. avoidance of restriction
6. breath of experience
7. aspects of physical environment
8. available play material

A significant difference was found between normal and malnutritious children with regard to their home environment. It differs in sub dimensions, the malnourished children had poor house environment in comparison to counterparts (Cravioto and Delicardie 1976). A low level of home stimulation and a passive traditional mother, unaware of the needs of her child, and responding to them in a minimal way as if unable to decode the infants signals, are two major characteristic features of poor micro environment that lead to severe mal nutrition in children of poor families (Reddy 1981; Rush 1984; Widdwson 1985).

The low concern of the child's need and health care with reference to malnutrition has been investigated systematically. Maternal anxiety / depression precipitated malnutrition produces several behavioural problems in children (Rahis and Cederblad 1986). Several other studies concluded that due to high tension in the family and absenteeism of father because of alcoholism induced the feeling of powerlessness amongst the mothers and that was found to be associated with malnutrition in children of those families (Lewis 1969; Callen 1971; Whorton 1982; Jarvos 1983; Mirsch 1987).

Salt *et al* (1988) studied the affects of maternal depressive symptoms and prevalence of mal nutrition in their children which was found clearly associated with growth retardation and increased behavioral problem in children of lower income group families.

A study by Rossetti(1978) entitled malnutrition and mother-infant asynchrony presents an explanation for the link between environment (micro level) malnutrition and mental development. The basic assumption in the study was that the biological factors (malnutrition) and socio-economic conditions interact to produce slow mental development. As a matter of fact, the malnourished children are less responsive towards the stimulation and future are being neglected by their parents.

Galler and Ramsay 1985) studied the children suffering from malnutrition. The results indicate that micro-environmental conditions (e.g. mother child relations, parental affection) were less favorable in malnourished subjects. Thus, poor maternal concern, fewer stimulating experience for the subjects (children), poor social relationships of the mother were more frequent in the mothers of malnourished children. Hence the lower maternal moral had significant impact on child growth (nutritional status) and behavioral problems.

Alvantez et al 1982 studied non verbal language in mother with malnourished infants and found that 90% of the mothers with malnourished infants had low degree of non verbal expression and 70% had low personal satisfaction with the families. Similar findings have been reported by Bhattacharya (1981).

The factors which affect the parenting qualities parent child relationship, and early childhood stimulation are highly associated with family characteristics, which directly or indirectly influence it and intern aggravate the problem of malnutrition and other associated health problems. Majority of the studies have taken the nature and type of family, income size and living conditions as determining factors of or malnutrition. However, no significant relationship was found between these characteristics of family and severe malnutrition, even so it can be stated that the family variables do not produce malnutrition directly but aggravate the problem when coupled with other micro-level factors like mother-child relationship, health status of mother, child rearing practices etc.

There are two objectives in investigating the relationship between micro level socio-cultural variables in malnutritional and growth and development. The first to understand the social process by which children become malnourished and subsequently have lower levels of intellectual function and behavioural problems. And the second objective is to determine with as great precision as possible the effects of malnutrition upon growth and development of a child separate from the effects of social environment.

The review of literature revealed that efforts have been made to examine the role of micro-level environment in prevalence of severe malnutrition in childhood; and as far as the role of micro-level environment is concerned maximum emphasis has been given on home environment, nature and type of family, family income, mother child interaction etc. A few studies have tried to explore the relationship between maternal psychological help and malnutrition. Since there are several factors; like family effective dynamics- in terms of interfamilial relationships, social support to the family and general well being of family. These are also the micro-level characteristics of family and may be associated with malnutrition in childhood. Studies have been carried on mother child interaction but the determining factor of mother-child interaction i.e. quality of parenting in terms of cordiality; protection and permissiveness have not been considered. The third factor psychosomatic health status of the mother has also some importance because it may hamper the family affective dynamics, quality of parenting and mother-child interaction and produce malnutrition and developmental disorders.

Emergence of Mental Health Problem: A Dynamic Model

In the light of recent and taxonomical research it has been clearly emerged that the quality of family effective dynamics and nature of parenting, if it is deficient produces mental health disorders among growing children Furthermore the children

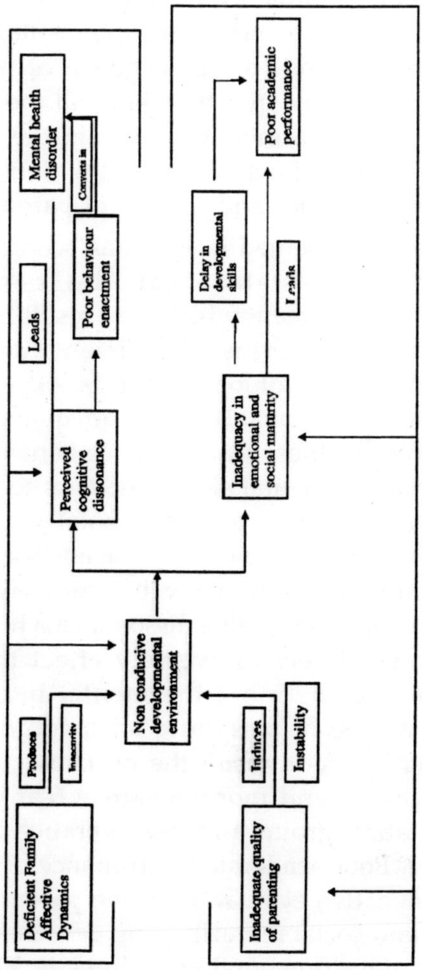

Fig. 1

with slight deviation found themselves in a non-conducive environment for their growth and development and as a result they further develop mental health problem. It is commonly observed that the children with deviant (mild) to disordered (marked) behavior are perceived as problematic children by the people present in and around their ultimate environment (Vidya and Tripathi;Tripathi 1992) The child's home environment in terms effective structure of his family and qualitative parenting influence his motivation intimately and consequently his behavior enactment and mental health status. It is our contention that the emergence of mental health problem has to be considered by taking all these factors into consideration. Fig.1 is a model to explain the emergence of mental health problem in children having deficiency in their family effective dynamics and quality of parenting.

The model as presented in fig.1 has been conceived as a dynamic model. It states that the non conducive developmental environment which may result from the forces operating at home in terms of deficient family effective dynamics and quality of parenting is likely to produce perceived cognitive dissonance and inadequacy in emotional and social maturity , these leads to poor behavior enactment and delay in developmental skills; needless to say child will find difficulty to acquire the positive mental and psychological status which is required for effective academic performance. Also, on account of inadequacy in emotional and social maturity the perceived cognitive dissonance which has already been acquired are likely to aversely effect the behavioral manifestations. Furthermore the mental health disorders influence the nature of parenting ad magnitude of family affective dynamics. As a result the psychological self of the child becomes more and more negative; fear of failure and negative reputation group and perseverance is likely to be weak and poor. Poor academic performance of the child also promotes the negative evaluation of the parent and hampers the emotional and social maturity thus, results in increasingly non conducive developmental environment. Therefore what may start out as a mildly non conducive developmental environment for a deviant child is likely to become more and more with the course of growth and development. As the pressure of the school become sever and the child find himself to cope with academic demand he is likely to take the first exit available to him, either by manifesting mild to marked mental health problem are by accepting the low self-esteem. The distinction in the model proposed and other available models lies in emphasizing the quality of parenting nature and magnitual of family affective dynamics and the effective role they play in the acquisition of behavioral strength and cognitive skills required for human being in adjusting with the environmental constrains in everyday life. It is generally said that the children with mental health problem with normal children differ with respect to various cognitive skills to began with poor cognitive skills responsible for their underachievement (Pande and Tripathi, 1981) Another study by Tripathi (1992) provides an ample proof that the qualitative family affective dynamics and quality parenting produces negative impact on behavior acquisition in early childhood. There is ample evidence in support of this model. Coleman's (1966) survey and findings of Pffeifer (1976) who found that the students having negative perceptions of the institutional preference also estimated their probability of success very low. It can, therefore, propagated that such individual will also be lower with respect to tendency to achieve success. The crucial factor, however, that contributes to cognitive dissonance about non conducive developmental environment has to do with the expectations of parents. Several studies have shown that parental expectancies and academic motivations are interrelated and interdependent. Once a child comes from deficient family affective dynamics and having inadequate quality of parenting starts perceiving that he is being taken negatively by his parents and other family members on account of discrepancy in interfamilial relationship social support to family, general well being of family members; cordiality, protection and permissiveness; it becomes difficult for him to emotionally and socially identify himself with his parents and peers. Generally there are few parents who take the early cognigence and try to facilitate the process of growth and development of their children otherwise the children is left to hi own devise to cook with existing environmental constrains.

The model also postulates that perceived cognitive dissonance in case of children having deficient family affective dynamics and quality of parenting will affect the behavioral enactment in general, negatively. This may happen in two ways. Firstly, it occurs due to perceived cognitive dissonance, the children with mild mental health problem may not feel courageous enough to put them in a socially desirable manner. This may happen due to restricted vocabulary and communication deficits. Another reason is that acquisition of poor academic performance depends on intellectual potential and emotional maturity (Tripathi and Vidya, 2003). In the absence of adequate emotional and social maturity proper growth and development and acquisition of cognitive potentials can not be proper which is the major contributor for academic performance and behavior enactments. Thus, the children with mental health problem face a double bind situation. They get pressure at home for academic activities and lack of opportunities for adequate growth and development of their personality; as a result they are left alone to acquire a mental health problem that is emergence of mental health problems caused by deficient family affective dynamics and inadequate quality of parenting.

REFERENCES

1. Alvarez, A. and Lee, A. (2004). Early forms of relatedness in autism: a longitudinal clinical and quantitative single case study. *Clinical Child Psychology and Psychiatry*, **9** (4), pp. 499-518.
2. *Birth Works – Primal Health Research Data Bank.* See: http://www.birthworks.org/primalhealth/

3. Bowlby, J. (1969). *Attachment: attachment and loss. Volume 1.* London: Pimlico.

4. Broidy, L. M., Nagin, D. S., Tremblay, R. E., et al. (2003). Developmental trajectories of childhood disruptive behaviors and adolescent delinquency: a six-site, cross-national study. *Developmental Psychology*, **39** (2), pp. 222-245.

5. Farrington, D. P. (1995). The development of offending and antisocial behaviour from childhood: key findings from the Cambridge study in delinquent development. *Journal of Child Psychology and Psychiatry and Allied Disciplines*, **360** (6), pp. 929-964.

6. Fonagy, P., Gergley, G., Jurist, E. L., et al. (2002). *Affect regulation, mentalization, and the development of the self.* New York: Other Press.

7. *Food and Behaviour Research.* See: http://www.fabresearch.org/

8. Gershoff, E. T. (2002). Corporal punishment by parents and associated child behaviors and experiences: a meta-analytic and theoretical review. *Psychological Bulletin*, **128** (4), pp. 539-579.

9. Gesch, C. B., Hammond, S. M., Hampson, S. E., et al. (2002). Influence of supplementary vitamins, minerals and essential fatty acids on the antisocial behaviour of young adult prisoners. *British Journal of Psychiatry*, **181** pp. 22-28.

10. Glaser, D. and Prior, V. (1997). Is the term child protection applicable to emotional abuse? *Child Abuse Review*, **6** (5), pp. 315-329.

11. Glaser, D. (2000). Child abuse and neglect and the brain: a review. *Journal of Child Psychology and Psychiatry*, **41** (1), pp. 97-116. Quotes from page 100 and 101.

9. Hagel, A. (2004). *Time trends in adolescent well-being.* London: Nuffield Foundation. See http://www.nuffieldfoundation.org/fileLibrary/pdf/04_seminars_children_families_adolescents_and_wellbeing.pdf

10. Hartley-Brewer, E. (2004). *Talking to twenties: getting it right before it gets rocky with your 8-12 year old.* London: Hodder and Stoughton

11. Huttunen, M. and Niskanen, P. (1978). Prenatal loss of father and psychiatric disorders. *Archives of General Psychiatry*, **35** (4), pp. 429-431.

12. Kim-Cohen, J., Caspi, A., Moffitt, T. E., et al. (2003). Prior juvenile diagnoses in adults with mental disorder: developmental follow-back of a prospective-longitudinal cohort. *Archives of General Psychiatry*, **60** (7), pp. 709-717.

13. Kochanska, G., Gross, J. N., Lin, M-H., et al. (2002). Guilt in young children: development, determinants, and relations with a broader system of standards. *Child Development*, **73** (2), pp. 461-482.

14. Meltzer, H., Gatward, R., Goodman, R., et al. (2000). *The Mental health of children and adolescents in Great Britain*. London: Stationery Office. See http://www.statistics.gov.uk/StatBase/Product.asp?vlnk=3983andPos=andColRank=1andRank=192

15. National Institute for Mental Health in England (NIMHE) (2005). *National suicide prevention strategy for England: Annual report on progresss.2004*.London: Department of Health. See http://www.dh.gov.uk/assetRoot/04/10/16/69/04101669.pdf

16. Rutter, M., Giller, H. and Hagel, A. (1998). *Antisocial behaviour by young people*. Cambridge: Cambridge University Press.

17. Rutter, M. and O'Connor, T. G. (2004). Are there biological programming effects for psychological development: findings from a study of Romanian adoptees. *Developmental Psychology*, **40** (1), pp. 81-94. http://content.apa.org/journals/dev/40/1/81

18. Strathearn, L., Li, J., Lanzi, R. G., *et al.* (2002). Personal Communication between Professor Fonagy and the authors.

19. Shively, C. A. (2000). Social status, stress, and health in female monkeys. In: Tarlov, A. R. and St. Peter, R. F. (eds.). *The society and population health reader: volume II: a state and community perspective*. New York: New Press.

20. Shively, C. A. (1998). Social subordination stress, behavior, and central monoaminergic function in female cynomolgus monkeys. *Biological Psychiatry*, **44** (9), pp. 882-891.

21. Shively, C. A., Laber-Laird, K. and Anton, R. F. (1997). Behavior and physiology of social stress and depression in female cynomolgus monkeys. *Biological Psychiatry*, **41** (8), pp. 871-882.

7

Gender Differences on Emotional Intelligence, Coping Strategies and Anxiety

Batool Pashang and Dr. Mridula Singh

Three studies were conducted to explore the gender differences on emotional intelligence, coping strategies and anxiety. A total of 599 adults between 20 to 50 years of age were selected randomly from Mysore city. Emotional Intelligence Scale, Coping checklist and Anxiety scale were administered to them all together. The results of the 't' test revealed that no significant difference between the male and female subjects on EI. However the findings from coping strategies disclosed no significant difference between the male and female subjects on Problem solving, Distraction positive, Distraction negative, Acceptance, Religion and Denial skills. On the other hand female adults used Social support skill more than those male. Further, results of the 't' test indicated that male subjects suffered from anxiety more that females.

When psychologists started to search and write about the intelligence, they focused on aspects, such as memory and problem-solving. However recently there are a number of psychologists who believe that the non-cognitive aspects such as emotions are also important. Salovey and Mayer introduced the concept of emotional intelligence for the first time in 1990. They defined it as "the ability to monitor one's own and others' feelings and emotions, to discriminate among them, and to use this information to guide one's thinking and actions". When we think about the human skills, we are faced with the question of gender difference. Goleman (1998) indicated that "there are no sex differences and women are not "smarter" than men when it comes to emotional intelligence, nor are men superior to women". Bar-On (1997) also mentioned that "EI is independent of sex". A study by Bansibihari and Pathan (2004) in India disclosed that Male and Female teachers did not differ in respect to other levels of Emotional intelligence. However Mandell and Pherwani (2004) verified no significant interaction between gender and emotional intelligence. The study by Brackett et al (2004) found that women were significantly higher than men in EI. Further, Petrides and Furnham (2006) described females, as being higher than males on the "social skills" factor of the measured trait EI. Psychologists make a distinction between two basic types of coping strategy - problem focused strategy and emotion focused strategy (Robinson, 2000). They propose that problem focused strategy, attempts to deal with those aspects of the environment that are responsible for the stress and anxiety experienced. It implies that in problem focused strategy the person deals directly with the stressful situation. While in emotion focused strategy attempts are made to change the way a person thinks about a stressful situation. Users of emotion focused strategy trying to deal with the emotional consequences of the stress rather than try to change the situation. Robinson (2000) pointed that an active problem focused strategy is often more effective in dealing with the anxiety because, changing the perception of the situation changes the way a person thinks anyway. Chosen coping strategy through problem focused or emotion focused mostly depends on the person and his traits. It seems a number of variables such as age, gender, culture and so on may affect an individual in dealing with the stressful situation.

Hoffman et al. (2004) evaluated gender differences in the relation between stressful life events and adjustment. They found that life events are associated among boys, but not girls, with increased anxiety and a trend toward heightened withdrawal. Women showed a preference for social strategies such as affiliating with others, to reduce anxiety (Campen and Roberts, 2001) and they had a more emotionally-oriented behavior, and men are said to be more problem-oriented (Ridder, 2000). Women use a proportionately greater amounts of confrontative coping, accepting responsibility, seeking social support and escape/avoidance when compare with men, whereas men use aproportionately greater amounts of distancing, self-controlling and planful problem-solving (Peterson et al. 2006). Females rated emotion-focused strategies as more effective with additional domain differences on problem-focused strategies and acceptance coping (Sigmon, Stanton and Snyder, 1995). Women scored significantly higher than men in emotional and avoidance coping styles, while scoring lower in relational and detachment coping styles (Matud, 2003). Further Kristoffersor et al. (2003) described that women use a variety of coping strategies such as minimizing the impact of the disease, tending to delay seeking treatment and not wanting to bother others with their health problems. Anxiety focuses on conceptualization of psychopathology, motivation, and personality, among the negative emotions which is the most widely experienced of all. Over the past two decades, there has been an increasing interest in studying the dimensions of the gender role, with much of this research being done to learn more about how the various components of gender role influence on people's physical and psychological well-being, as well as their interactions with others. In a practical work Muris et al. (2005) disclosed that gender role orientation accounted for more of the variance in fear and anxiety scores than men. Jones et al. (2002) found no gender differences in pain tolerance or pain intensity but they recognized gender differences in pain threshold in the anxiety group, contrary to past findings, females showed significantly higher pain thresholds than males. Diagnosis of depression was significantly correlated with female gender, age under 50 years, and higher average scores on trait anxiety and state anxiety. Depressed men were usually younger than 50 years of age, smokers and having a higher average score on trait anxiety and state anxiety than those non-depressed (Perez et al. 2005).

In the light of the above discussion, it may seem worthwhile to examine the following objectives:

- To find out the gender differences on emotional intelligence.
- To find out the gender differences on aspects of emotional intelligence.
- To determine the gender differences on coping strategies.
- To determine the gender differences on anxiety.
- To determine the gender differences on traits of anxiety.

Hypotheses

1) There is a significant difference between male and female subjects on emotional intelligence.

2) There is a significant difference between male and female subjects on coping strategies.

3) There is a significant difference between male and female subjects on anxiety.

Measures

The following assessment instruments were employed in this study:

First, the Emotional Intelligence Scale (EIS) developed by Anukool Hyde and Sanjyot Pathe in 2001. This instrument is made of 34 items and provides an indicator of the levels of perceived EI. Respondents are asked to rate their degree of agreement of the items on a 5-point Likert- type scale ranging from 1 (strongly disagree) to 5 (strongly agree). EIS has 10 subscales. The subscales are self awareness, self motivation, self development, empathy, emotional stability, managing relations, integrity, value orientation, commitment, and altruistic behavior. Next, the Coping check list (CCL) developed by Kiran Rao, Subbakrishna, D.K. and Prabhu in 1989. The CCL had 7 subscales developed on priority basis and validated in normal, adult, community sample. There was one problem focused scale (Problem Solving), 5 Emotion-focused scale (Distraction Positive methods, Distraction Negative methods, Acceptance, Religion and Denial), and the last one was of Social Support which is a combination of both problem and focused coping. Last, the Anxiety Scale (IPAT) developed by R.B.Cattel, S.E.Krug and H.Scleier in 1976. IPAT is a 40 items Questionnaire and provide a convenient and practical measure of anxiety traits. Traits of anxiety namely, Emotional instability, Suspiciousness, Guilt proneness, Low integration and Tension.

Statistical Analyses

In order to analyse the gender differences on aspects of Emotional intelligence,'t' test technique was employed.

Procedure

A sample of 599 adults (male=299 and female=300), between the ages of 20 to 50 were selected from Mysore City. The EI scale, Coping checklist and Anxiety scale were administered to them together. Maximum care was taken to see that no item was omitted and respondents were assured that their individual results would be kept confidential.

Results

In order to verify the stated hypothesis, the "t" test was employed. Tables 1, 2 and 3 present the descriptive statistics as well as results of the "t" test for the studied variables in the present sample of subjects. The results are described below for each of the research questions.

Gender Differences and EI

The results of the t-test obtained on EI (Table 1) revealed that the t-value of male and female subjects on EI was (t=1.70) and the significance was (.09). As 0.05 and below denotes significant difference, it is evident from the Table 1 that both groups (Male/ Female) do not show any significant difference on Emotional intelligence.

TABLE - 1

Comparison between Male and Female subjects with respect to EI and EI factors

Variables	*Sex*	*Mean*	*SD*	*t.value*	*p.value*	*Result*
Self awareness	F	16.26	3.01	-.28	.78	Non
(EIA)	M	16.33	2.99			significant
Empathy	F	17.65	3.48	1.54	.12	Non
(EIB)	M	17.20	3.68			significant
Self motivation	F	21.91	4.18	2.39	.02	Significant
(EIC)	M	21.00	5.08			
Emotional	F	14.72	2.97	.27	.79	Non
stability (EID)	M	14.65	3.33			significant
Managing	F	14.93	2.99	1.45	.15	Non
Relation (EIE)	M	14.58	2.90			significant
Integrity	F	11.79	2.53	-.81	.42	Non
(EIF)	M	11.98	2.83			significant
Self development	F	7.75	1.67	2.83	.00	Significant
(EIG)	M	7.35	1.89			
Value orientation	F	7.51	1.66	2.44	.01	Significant
(EIH)	M	7.19	1.63			
Commitment	F	7.46	1.66	.51	.61	Non
(EII)	M	7.39	1.63			significant
Altruisticbehavior	F	7.38	1.78	.87	.38	Non
(EIJ)	M	7.26	1.73			significant
EI	**F**	**127.54**	**17.96**	**1.70**	**.09**	**Non**
(Total)	**M**	**124.92**	**19.69**			**significant**

Note - N=599

The results of the t-test obtained on EI factors (Table 1) revealed that the t-value of male and female subjects on Self awareness (EIA) was (t=-.28) and the significance was (.78), for Empathy (EIB) was (t=1.54) and the significance was (.12), for Emotional stability(EID) was (t=.27) and the significance was (.79), for Managing relations (EIE) was (t=1.45) and the significance was (.15), for Integrity (EIF) was (t=-.81) and the significance was (.42), for Commitment (EII) was (t=.51) and the significance was (.61), for Altruistic behavior (EIJ) was (t=.87) and the significance was (.38). As 0.05 and below denotes significant difference, it is evident from the Table 1 that both groups (Male/ Female) do not show any significant difference on Self awareness, Empathy, Emotional stability, Managing relations, Integrity, Commitment and Altruistic behavior.

On the other hand the results of the t-test on EI factors (Table 1) revealed that the t-value of male and female subjects on Self motivation (EIC) was (t=2.39) and the significance was (.02). Therefore it is evident from Table 1 that there is a significant difference between the male and female groups in Self motivation. The mean values (Table 1) revealed that the females had (M=21.91, SD=4.18) higher score than males (M=21, SD=5.08) on EIC. Significant Self development (EIG) was (t=2.83) and the p-value was (.00). Therefore it is evident from the Table 1 that there is a significant difference between the male and female groups on Self development (EIG). The mean values (Table 1) revealed that females had (M=7.75, SD=1.67) higher score than males (M=7.35, SD=1.81) on EIG. Significant Value orientation (EIH) was (t=2.44) and the p-value was (.01). Therefore it is evident from Table 1 that there is a significant difference between the male and female groups on value orientation. The mean values (Table 1) revealed that females had (M=7.51, SD=1.66) higher score than males (M=7.19, SD=1.63) on EIH.

Gender Difference and Coping Strategies

The results of the t-test obtained on Coping strategies (Table 2) revealed that the t-value of male and female subjects on Problem solving (PS) was (t=1.25) and the significance was (.21), for Distraction positive (DP) was (t=.95) and the significance was (.34), for Distraction negative (DN) was (t=-1.13) and the significance was (.26), for Acceptance (AC), was (t=1.17) and the significance was (.24), for Religion (RE) was (t=.66) and the significance was (.51), for Denial (DE) was (t=-.60) and the significance was (.11). As 0.05 and below denotes significant difference, it is evident from the Table 2 that the male and female subjects did not differ significantly on Problem solving, Distraction positive, Distraction negative, Acceptance, Religion, Denial Coping strategies.

TABLE - 2

Comparison between Male and Female subjects with respect to Coping strategies

Variables	*Sex*	*Mean*	*SD*	*t.value*	*p.value*	*Result*
Problem solving (PS)	F M	6.05 5.81	2.14 2.40	1.25	.210	Non significant
Distraction positive (DP)	F M	7.08 6.81	3.34 3.71	.95	.343	Non significant
Distraction negative (DN)	F M	4.47 4.71	2.58 2.56	-1.13	.257	Non significant
Acceptance (AC)	F M	6.40 6.17	2.35 2.48	1.17	.242	Non significant
Religion (RE)	F M	5.24 5.13	1.97 2.25	.66	.509	Non significant
Denial (DE)	F M	4.86 5.16	2.19 2.34	-1.60	.109	Non significant
Social support (SS)	**F** **M**	**4.07** **3.74**	**1.55** **1.65**	**2.55**	**.011**	**Significant**

Note - N=599

On the other hand the results of the t-test obtained on Coping strategies (Table 2) revealed that the t-value of male and female subjects on Social support (SS) was (t=2.55) and the significance was (.01). Therefore it is evident from Table 2 that there is a significant difference between the male and female groups on Social support. The mean values (Table 2) revealed that females had (M=4.07, SD=1.55) higher score than males (M=3.73, SD=1.65) on SS.

Gender Difference and Anxiety Traits

The results of the t-test obtained on Anxiety (Table 3) revealed that the t-value of male and female subjects on Anxiety was (t=-2.85) and the p-value was (.00). Therefore it is evident from the Table 3 that there was a significant difference between the male and female groups on Anxiety. The mean values (Table 3) revealed that the males (M=6.73, SD=1.02) scored higher than females (M=6.47, SD=1.21) on Anxiety.

TABLE - 3

Comparison between Male and Female subjects with respect to Anxiety and Traits of anxiety

Variables	*Sex*	*Mean*	*SD*	*t.value*	*p.value*	*Result*
Low self control (Q3)	F	5.87	3.00	-1.75	.081	Non significant
	M	6.35	3.60			
Emotional Instability (C)	F	5.46	2.73	-1.89	.059	Significant
	M	5.90	2.93			
Suspicion (L)	F	5.04	1.67	-8.45	.000	Significant
	M	6.20	1.69			
Apprehension (0)	F	9.82	2.89	12.43	.000	Significant
	M	6.98	2.7			
Tension (Q4)	F	8.04	2.01	-.01	.990	Non significant
	M	8.05	3.11			
Total Anxiety	**F**	**6.47**	**1.21**	**-2.85**	**.005**	**Significant**
	M	**6.73**	**1.03**			

Note - N=599

The results of the t-test obtained on Anxiety traits (Table 3) revealed that the t-value of male and female subjects on Low self control (Q3) was (t=-1.75) and the significance was (.08), and for Tension (Q4) was (t=-.01) and the significance was (.99). As 0.05 and below denotes significant difference, it is evident from the Table 3 that both male and female groups did not differ significantly on Low self control and Tension traits.

On the other hand the results of the t-test obtained on Anxiety traits (Table 3) revealed that the t-value of male and female subjects on Emotional instability (C) was (t=-1.89) and the significance was (.05). Therefore it is evident from Table 3 that there is a significant difference between the male and female groups on Emotional instability trait. The mean values (Table 3) revealed that males had (M=5.90, SD=2.93) higher score than females (M=5.46, SD=2.73) on C. Significant Suspicion (L) was (t=-8.45) and the significance was (.00). Therefore it is evident from Table 3 that there is a significant difference between the male and female groups on Suspicion trait. The mean values (Table 3) revealed that males had (M=6.2, SD=1.69) higher score than females (M=5.04, SD=1.67) on L. Significant Apprehension (O) was (t=12.43) and the significance was (.00). Therefore it is evident from Table 3 that there is a significant difference between the male and female groups on Apprehension trait. The mean values (Table 3) revealed that females had (M=9.82, SD=2.89) higher score than males (M=6.98, SD=2.7) on Apprehension trait.

Discussion

In the present study males and females were compared on all the tasks of the Emotional intelligence, Coping strategies and Anxiety. The results are discussed below for each of the research questions.

Gender Differences in Relation to Emotional Intelligence

The hypothesis that male and female differ in their EI was not supported by the present study findings. The studies by Bar-on (1997) had supported these findings. Goleman (1998) also indicated that there was no difference between males and females on EI. Other studies by Bansibihari and Pathan, (2004), verified that the Male and Female teachers did differ in respect of the other levels of Emotional intelligence. On the other hand, Mandell and Pherwani (2004) noted that females had a higher EI than males and Katyal and Awasthi, (2005) verified that girls scored higher in emotional intelligence than boys. These findings were not in line with the results of the present study. The reasons for the difference could be that in those studies, females were self-enhancing and males self-derogating. Regarding EI factors, the results clearly indicated that females scored marginally higher than males on Self motivation, Self development and Value orientation. It is therefore clear that despite evidence that females seem to be equal with males on EI levels, their Self motivation, Self development and Value orientation scores tend to be marginally higher than those of the males. As Petrides and Furnham (2004) found, gender bias is extended to tests of self-estimation of EI. While some studies, such as Neera & Anand (2004), Brackett et al (2004), Henry et al, (2001) and Petrides and Furnham (2006) indicated that there are very few significant differences between the two groups (male and female) in EI traits, the results of their study verified that there was no significant difference between both of the groups in Self awareness, Empathy, Emotional stability, Managing relations, and Integrity, Commitment and Altruistic behavior. Hence the lack of gender differences might possibly be due to the nature of scoring utilized or sample situation.

Gender Differences in Relation to Coping Strategies

The hypothesis that males and females differ in Problem solving, Distraction positive, Distraction negative, Acceptance, Religion and Denial strategies, was not supported by the present research findings. Studies by Hooker et al. (2000) showed different results; care giving wives were less likely than husbands, to use problem-focused coping strategies. The other study by Ridder (2000), found that women have a more emotionally-oriented behavior, while men are said to be more problem-oriented. Peterson et al. (2006) also found that men used proportionately greater amounts of distancing, self-controlling and planful problem-solving. Another aspect focusing on the different coping strategies of men and women is the difference in using Distraction positive and Acceptance strategies. Studies by Sigmon et al. (1995), indicated that females rated emotion-focused strategies as being more effective with additional domain differences on problem-focused strategies and acceptance coping. In family situations females rated problem-solving as more effective and rated acceptance coping strategies as being more effective in coping in a stressful relationship than males. However these findings are different from results of the present study, this could be due to the coping behaviors, not being good or bad in themselves, but the situation in which they are used could make them effective or ineffective. The other reason might be that, now a days both sexes try to be similar in all work. Most of the participants in the sample of the present study were students' between ages 20-25, really young with new ideas. The mean scores of the present study showed that females used social support strategy more than males. Studies by Campen and Roberts (2001), verified that females showed a preference for social strategies, such as affiliating with others, to reduce anxiety. Also Peterson et al. (2006), found that women used seeking 'social support' far more when compared with men. Studies have been shown to support these findings. On the other hand a few studies such as Hooker et al. (2000) indicated that there are no significant gender differences in either group for social support or emotion-focused coping did not supporting the findings of the study. The reason may lie in the nature of situations and samples which were different. As already mentioned, the results of the study displayed that males and females used Distraction negative, Denial and Religion strategies equally. These findings are not supported by some studies such as Matud (2003), who found that women scored significantly higher than men in emotional and avoidance coping styles, and Bischof et al (2005), observed that male alcohol-dependent individuals reported a higher temptation to drink in positive situations, and female alcohol-dependent individuals who reported a higher educational level, also displayed a higher degree of temptation to drink. The reason might lie in the cultural differences between the samples.

Gender Differences in Relation to Anxiety

The hypothesis that males and females differ in their anxiety was supported by the present research findings. These observations are in line with Jones et al. (2002), who argued that there are gender differences in pain threshold in anxiety, with females showing a significantly higher pain threshold than males. The other study by Hoffman et al (2004) also claimed that life events were associated among boys, but not girls, with increased anxiety and a trend towards heightened withdrawal. As already mentioned regarding the traits of anxiety, there were significant differences between both groups. Males scored higher than females in Emotional instability and Suspicion than those females in the present study. On the other hand women suffered from Apprehension more than men. The studies by Perez et al. (2005), which referred to gender differences, supported these findings.

REFERENCES

Bansibihari, P., Pathan, Y.G. (2004). Emotional intelligence secondary teachers. *Edutracks,* December, 2004.

Bar-on, R. (1997). *Emotional Quotient Inventory (EQ-I) Multi-Health Systems, Technical Manual.* Toronto, Canada

Brackett, M.B., Mayer, J.D., Warner, R.M. (2004). Emotional intelligence and its relation to everyday behavior. *Personality and Individual Differences,* 36, 387–1402.

Goleman, D. (1998). *Working with Emotional Intelligence.* New York: Bantam.

Henry, R.B., Nanette, M.H.,Michael H, Gibbon, T. (2001). The relation of LD and gender with emotional intelligence in college students. *Journal of learning disabilities.* 34, 66-78.

Katyal, S., Awasthi, E. (2005). Gender Differences in Emotional Intelligence. *Journal of Psychology*. May 12, 2005, from: www.springerlink.com.

Mandell, B., Pherwani, S. (2004). Relationship Between Emotional Intelligence and Transformational Leadership Style: A Gender Comparison. *Journal of Busines and Psychology*. Retrieved November 2, 2004, from: www.springerlink.com.

Neera, P., Anand, P. (2004). Multe-factor Emotional Intelligence Scale (MEIS). *National Academy of Psychology, India,* 49, 2-3.

Petrides, K.V., Furnham,A. (2006). The Role of Trait Emotional Intelligence in a Gender-Specific Model of Organizational Variables. *Journal of applied social psychology,* 36, 552.

Salovey, P., and Mayer, J. D. (1990). Emotional intelligence. *Imagination, Cognition, and Personality, 9,* 185-211.

Bischof, G., Rumpf, H.J., Meyer, C., Hapke, U., John, U. (2005). Gender differences in temptation to drink, self-efficacy to abstain and coping behavior in treated alcohol- dependent individuals: Controlling for severity of dependence. *Addiction Research and Theory,* Retrieved April 5, 2005, from: www. Taylor and Francis.com.

Campen, C., Roberts, D.C. (2001). Coping Strategies of Runners: Perceived Effectiveness and Match to Precompetitive Anxiety. *Journal of Sport Behavior,* 24, 18-22.

Hoffman, M.A., Shiff, R.L., Ushpiz, V. (2004). Gender differences in the relation between stressful life events and adjustment among school-aged children. *Sex Rules*. October 22, 2004, from: www.springerlink.com.

Hooker, K., Manoogian, M., Monahan, D.J., Frazier, L.D., Shifren, K. (2000). Gender Differences Among Alzheimer's and Parkinson's Disease Spouse Caregivers. *The Gerontological Society of America*. 16, 25-27.

Kristofferzon, M.L., Löfmark, R., Carlsson,M. (2003). Gender differences in coping and social support. *Journal of Advanced Nursing*. 44, 360.

Matud, M. P. (2003). Gender differences in stress and coping styles. *Journal of Personality and Individual Differences*. 37, 1401-1415.

Peterson, B.D., Newton, C.R., Rosen, K.H., Skaggs, G.E. (2006). Gender differences in how men and women who are referred for IVF cope with infertility stress. *Oxford Journals*, 21, 12-14.

Rao, K., Subbakrishna, D.K. and Prabhu, G.G. (1989). Development of a coping checklist: A preliminary report . *Indian Journal of Psychology*, 31, 128-133.

Robinson, D. (2000). *101 Key Ideas - Psychology.* London: Hodder and Stoughton.

Sigmon, S.T., Stanton, L., Snyder, C.R. (1995). Gender differences in coping, Health and Fitness. *Sex Roles: A Journal of research.* Retrieved November 3, 1995, from: www.findarticles.com

Ridder, D. (2000). Gender, stress and coping: Do women handle stressful situations differently from men? . *Women, health and the mind.* England: Wiley. Pp. 115-135.

Hoffman, M.A., Shiff, R.L., Ushpiz, V. (2004). Gender differences in the relation between stressful life events and adjustment among school-aged children. *Sex Rules.* October 22, 2004, from: www.springerlink.com.

Jones, A., Spindler, H., Jørgensen, M.M., Zachariae, R. (2002).The effect of situation-evoked anxiety and gender on pain report using the cold press or test Scandinavian. *Journal of Psychology*. 43, 307.

Muris, P., Meestrs, C., Knoops, K. (2005). The Relation Between Gender Role Orientation and Fear and Anxiety in Nonclinic-Referred Children. *Journal of Clinical Child and Adolescent Psychology*. 34, 326-332.

Perez, G.H., Nicolau, J.C., Romano, B.W., Laranjeira, R. (2005). Arquivos Brasileiros de Cardiologia, Arq. *Bras Cardio.* 85, 5

8

Burnout and Anger in Teachers and Parents
Implications for child Development

Aley, V.A.

This study is an attempt to understand how burnout and anger in teachers and parents affect the development of children. 45 teachers, who are also parents, from two different schools served as sample. The tools used were (1) Maslach Burnout Inventory- Human Services Survey (3rd Edition 1996), (2) Self-Monitoring Form for Anger and Life Experiences Questionnaire (Kassinove, H. and Tafrate, C.R., 2002). 20 per cent of the sample fell under the "High" range category on Emotional Exhaustion, and 40 per cent " High" on Diminished personal accomplishment and only 10 per cent " High" on Depersonalization. The intensity of emotional arousal experienced during anger experience ranged from 40 to 90 on a scale of 1-100, on the life experiences questionnaire. 30 Persons out of the 45 recorded " headache" as the main physical symptom during or after the anger experience. Results of the study, limitations, and recommendations for further study and suggestions for mitigating the effects of burnout and anger are discussed. Possible strategies for improving the emotional health of teachers and parents are also dealt with.

An Overview of Literature on Burnout and Anger

BURNOUT

"Burnout can be described as a chronic state of exhaustion due to long term interpersonal stress within human service professions. It pertains to feelings experienced by people whose jobs require repeated exposure to emotionally charged social situations."(Shwarzer et al., 1999). Cherniss (1980) has defined burnout "as negative personal changes that occur over time in helping professionals who work in demanding or frustrating jobs." He proposed a process model that focused on stress and coping experiences resulting in negative attitude change. According to this model, certain work settings interact with individual differences. Individuals cope with these stresses in different ways. Some respond to employ strategies such as problem solving, whereas others respond by exhibiting negative attitude changes, that is Burnout. This is a kind of avoidant, resignative coping process that leads to reduced well being and reduced accomplishments (Burk and Greenglass, 1995).

Burnout also has been defined as a " syndrome of Emotional Exhaustion, Depersonalization, and Reduced Accomplishment, which is a special risk for individuals who work with other people in some capacity" (Leiter and Maslach, 1998,p.347). Emotional Exhaustion is seen as the stress component. It refers to feelings of being emotionally over extended and depleted of one's emotional resources. Fatigue, debilitation, loss of energy and wearing out are characteristics of this component. Depersonalization is the " other evaluation Component." It is described as cynicism, irritability, loss of idealism, and negative or inappropriate attitudes toward recipients. It also refers to a negative, callous or excessively detached response to other people. Reduced personal accomplishment is the " self evaluation content " and is equated with reduced personal efficacy , productivity or capability, low morale, and an inability to cope with job demands .It represents a decline in one's feelings of competence and achievement at work.

Burnout can be conceived as a process. The most widely used Maslach Burnout Inventory (MBI; Maslach et al., 1996) refers to "syndrome" which develops an over long term stressful encounters. Inadequate coping responses to the stressful encounters may lead to emotional exhaustion .In order to avoid becoming more and more exhausted people withdraw from their clients and start focusing on their private life. Distancing oneself from one's job then can lead to reduced accomplishment on the job.

DeFrank and Stroup (1989) indicate that the teaching has been associated with significant levels of burnout. Researchers have attempted to identify stressors in the teaching environment. These include workload, role ambiguity and conflict, pressures of the teacher's role, inadequate resources, poor working conditions, lack of professional recognition ,low remuneration, lack of involvement in decision making, lack of effective communication , staff conflicts, and pupil misbehaviour (Boyle et al., 1995; Pithers and Forgarty, 1995; Pithers and Soden ,1998). These occupational stressors have been associated with higher levels of Burnout, distress, depression, and absenteeism,

(Griffith, Steptoe and Cropley, 1999; Mazur and Lynch , 1989; Pierce and Molloy, 1990). Studies also suggest that stressors which cause teacher stress, and in turn burnout, are the result of external factors and individual dispositions (Watson and Clark, 1984), cognitive appraisal (Lazarusand Folkman, 1984), and other personal and social resources. (Van Dickand Wagner, 2001). Lerner, E.A. (2002) did a study on the experience of burnout among helping professionals in India .in relationship to extraversion and the entire network of social support. Participants were 134 helping professionals trained at the Christian Counselling Centre, Vellore. Results indicated that extraverts reported less burnout than introverts, particularly with respect to their sense of personal accomplishment.

ANGER

Kassinove and Sukhodolsky (1995) defined anger "as a felt emotional state."

They maintain that "this private state varies in intensity and duration as well as frequency and is associated with cognitive distortions verbal, motor behaviours, and patterns of physical arousal. Although anger may emerge spontaneously when another person is typically seen as the cause of anger. And it usually includes a perception of blameworthiness.

According to Kassinove Anger is not a form of aggression, and most often doesn't lead to Aggression! Rather it is a felt experience that typically follows unwanted, aversive interactions with close friends, colleagues, and family members. Although anger is common and sometimes useful, it can become an independent problem with many negative consequences, requiring treatment in the context of individuals, couples or family therapy in private practice or institutional settings. According to constructivists, 'anger is a role or a socially constructed, reinforced behavioural script ' that we learn to play. It consists of private thoughts, physiological reactions, and observable verbal and motor behaviours (e.g. Averill, 1982, 1983; Wessler, 1992).

Emotional responses have been acknowledged as playing a formative role in parenting including maladaptive parenting processes. (Dix, 1991). Presumably, anger is a high frequency, high intensity emotion experienced by parents during their caretaking role. In fact anger toward children is becoming recognized as a common emotional experience in parent-child interactions (Peterson et al., 1994) as well as an identified high risk behaviour frequently associated with forceful parent-child interactions (e.g. Kolko 1996). Findings suggest that parents' uncontrolled anger toward their children is strongly associated with child physical abuse (e.g. Kolko, 1996; Novaco, 1975; Vatsa 1982).

Rodriguez and Green (1997) highlight the importance and relevance of anger expression to the study of physical child abuse. Their findings revealed that anger expression and parenting stress combined to child abuse potential (i.e. characteristics and attitudes associated with child abuse) better than either factor alone. (Rodriguez and Green, 1997).

Limited parental self control or harsh discipline, such as heightened anger has been noted as a high risk factor warranting ongoing assessment (Kolko, 1996). In an examination of the relationship between anger and other correlates of abusive parenting, Peterson et al., (1994) found that mothers' self report of child behaviours which elicited the most anger resulted in the highest anger scores as well as the highest use of physical discipline. Similarly, Dukewich et al., (1996) found predisposition for aggressive coping to be a significant mediating variable of the effects of expectations about child development and limited parenting skills on one's potential for child abuse. Bauer and Twentyman (1985) found that abusive mothers possess unrealistic expectations of their children's behaviour and report being more annoyed with their children's behaviour when compared with non-abusive mothers. In his review of the literature on abusive parent characteristics, Wolfe (1987) found that abusive parents, relative to their non-abusive counterparts, tend to have a low frustration tolerance, which may contribute to heightened levels of parental anger. Further, abusive and non-abusive parents, have been found to differ along various dimensions including coping with anger provoking situations (e.g. Hansen et al., 1995). However although this research addresses emotional and coping responses that may be related to anger, there is limited research involving direct assessment of anger across various parenting situations.

The growing body of research examining the role of parental anger in negative parent child interactions and potentially harmful parenting behaviours also highlights parental anger as a key variable for monitoring the clinical course of maltreating families in treatment. However, paper assessment of this construct has received insufficient empirical examination. Although parental anger has been implicated in coercive and abusive parenting practices (e.g. Mckay et al., 1996), such conclusions are often based on assumption about the relationship between anger and aggressive parental acts rather than actual assessment of such experiences. Thus a discrepancy exists between the field's emphasis on parental anger and its relationship to harmful parenting behaviour (e.g.maltreating situations) and the availability and use of adequate tools to assess this specific type of anger. As parental anger is becoming increasingly recognized as a central aspect of parenting there is a need for more sensitive and specific assessment of this construct. Given that links between reported anger and subsequent parental behaviour have been demonstrated, assessment of parental anger seems to be a key component of prevention and intervention efforts arrived at maltreating or the other distressed parents who may be at future risk for engaging in maltreatment. Specifically, objective and standardized measures of parenting specific anger have been noticeably lacking in assessment protocols used with maltreating, help seeking, and other distressed parents. This shortage most likely explains the use of internally developed anger measures (e.g. within a specific research programme) on global measures of anger and stress.(e.g. Novaco Anger control Scale, Hassels Scale) by researchers and practitioners.

One such measure, the Parental anger inventory (PAI; Mac Millan et al., 1988) has been specifically developed to meet this need .It is worth mentioning that a study was done by Sedlar G. and Hansen D.J., (2001) to evaluate the Parental Anger Inventory (PAI) developed to measure specifically parental anger in response to child misbehaviour. Results support the internal consistency, temporal stability, and convergent validity of the Parental Anger Inventory (PAI).

Tools Used

Maslach's Burnout Inventory – Human Services Survey Self Monitoring Form for Anger and Life Experiences Questionnaire (Kassinove and Tafrate).

Methodology

Selection of sample was purposive i.e., Teachers who are also parents from two different schools in Vellore were selected. The MBI- Human services Survey and the self-monitoring form were administered on the same day in a group setting in the school premises with the cooperation of the principals.

Sample

The sample in this study consisted of 45 teachers, 40 females, and 5 males and their average age was 41. All of them were parents of children in the school going age. 26 were junior school teachers and 3 were junior school incharges of the same school. 16 were senior school teachers of a different school.

Procedure

The investigator went to the two schools, met the principals and administered the inventory and the questionnaires after clear instructions to the group. This was done in the school premises.

Results

TABLE - 1

Burnout Components	High (%)	Average (%)	Low (%)
Emotional Exhaustion (EE)	20	29	51
Depersonalization (DP)	10	20	70
Diminished Personal Accomplishment (PA)	40	26	34

N = 45

TABLE - 2

Burnout Components	High	Average Anger Score
Emotional Exhaustion (EE)	20%	35%
Depersonalization (DP)	10%	54%
Diminished Personal Accomplishment (PA)	40%	69%

N = 45

Discussion

The percentages of the sample high on the three components of Burnout are shown in Table - 1. 40% of the sample reported high on diminished personal accomplishment, this is indicative of a lack of sense of achievement which shows some effect of burnout. It is interesting to note that only 10% of the sample are high on depersonalization and only 20% reported high on emotional exhaustion. Depersonalization causes one to treat the recipients as objects, meaning they become callous, insensitive to the feelings of others. Perhaps the word " Depersonalization" brings up a sense of shock to those persons who feel that they need to be peaceful all the time. The variables of culture and social desirability could have played a role in this study.

Table 2 shows average anger intensity scores in percentages for this group. Correlation between Burnout measures and anger scores were not significant. In this study a high percentage (75%) of the teachers reported " Headache" during and after the anger experience. This points towards psychosomatic implications. Unrecognized and unexpressed feelings get somatized. "Headache is a common symptom a conversion reaction where anxiety from an unconscious conflict is converted into a physical symptom". The most common type of psychogenic headache is psychosomatic or psycho-physiological where longstanding emotional stresses produce changes in the vasculature or muscles to produce headache. It is also interesting to note that the 25% of the sample experienced rapid heart rate, sweating and fatigue and energy loss. (Verghese, A. and Abraham, A., 1996). "Emotional stresses produce changes in the various systems of the body e.g. blood pressure goes up; pulse rate increases, respiration becomes deep and prolonged. Muscle tension increases: sweat gland activity increases: mouth becomes dry; gastric acidity is raised; intestinal motility increases"(Verghese,A. and Abraham, A., 1996). What is conscious we can take charge of while what is unconscious takes charge of us! Perhaps our cultural upbringing where anger is a prohibited emotion to a certain extent, is an intervening variable.

Many teachers mentioned beating their children in order to make them obey or to bring about discipline. Once again physical abuse of children is an indicator of anger and frustration. Stressed out teacher parents have a double emotional burden to carry. Snapping responses, shouting and screaming at children are some other ways in which this group expresses their anger often.

Implications for the Emotional Health of Teachers and Parents

Since we want children to develop in a healthy way, it is important that we help parents and teachers to deal with their anger. The various steps in dealing with anger need to be emphasized, namely, (1) becoming aware of one's anger. (2) accepting and taking responsibility for one's anger (3) expressing one's anger constructively, i.e. without damage to people and property. In the case of teachers and parents, anger that is an aftermath of Burnout would call for action to counteract existing burnout and prevent potential burnout. Individual and Organizational strategies for stress reduction are needed.

Schools and colleges need to have an atmosphere of teamwork among the principals and staff, staff and students and students among themselves. Teachers need to be listened to and they in turn need to listen to the students. Teachers and parents need to use the skills of empathetic listening. Communication Skills need to become a part of staff training and student curriculum. If anger is a result of low self-esteem programmes to improve the self-esteem it need to be incorporated in to the school situation. More importance need to be given to Emotional Intelligence which will help constructive development of children into healthy adults. The different schools of psychotherapy, namely, Psychodynamic therapy, Behaviour therapy, Rational Emotive therapy and Neuro-Linguistic Programming can provide valuable tools for improving the mental health of the teachers and parents. On a sociological plane this calls for collaboration between various professionals in the psychological and educational field to make the future generation healthy and enjoying life with a sense of well being.

Limitations of the Study

The sample size was inadequate and no mediating factor was incorporated. The numbers of women and men in the sample were 40 and 5. Other mediating variables were not incorporated.

Recommendations for further Study

This study opens up many avenues for further research. Conducting this study on a larger sample in a different cultural setting, in another Northern State or with another cultural group may bring about varying and interesting results. The gender factor too counts since the socialization of the male is very different from that of the female in almost all the states in India. Self reporting by persons who are not aware of their own feelings and those who would not want to acknowledge their genuine feelings make a great difference, hence it is important to do a more purposive selection to eliminate all these influences. It is also important to incorporate other mediating variables like, coping styles and social support. Autocratic atmosphere in the school also could have brought about conscious response suppression.

REFERENCES

Maslach, C., Jackson, S.E. and Leiter ,M.P.(1996). Maslach Burnout inventory Manual (3rd edn.). Palo Alto , CA : Consulting Psychologists Press.

Kassinove , H and Tafrate, C. (2002). Anger Management . Impact Publishers,Inc. Atascadero, California.

Schwarzer, R. Schmitz, G. and Tang , C.(1999) Anxiety, Stress, and Coping, Vol.13, pp. 309-326.

Cherniss, C. (1980). Professional Burnout in Human Service Organizations. New York : Praeger .

Burke, R.J., Greenglass, E. (1995). A longitudinal study of psychological burnout in teachers. Human Relations, 48, 187-202.

Leiter ,M.P.andMaslach, C.(1998). Burnout In H.S. Friedman(Ed)., Encyclopedia of Mental Health (Vol.1,pp.347-357). New York : Academic Press.

DeFrank , R.S., and Stroup,C.A. (1989). Teacher stress and health: Examination of a model. Journal of Psychosomatic Research, 33,99-109.

Boyle, G.J., Borg, M.G., Falzon , J.M., and Baglioni, A.J. (1995). A Structural model of dimensions of teacher stress. British Journal of Educational Psychology, 65, 49-67.

Pithers, R.T., and Forgarty, G.J. (1995). Occupational stress among vocational teachers. British Journal of Educational Psychology, 65, 3-14.

Pithers , R.T., and Soden, R. (1998) Scottish and Australian Teacher stress and strain: A comparative study . British Journal of Educational Psychology, 68, 269-279.

Griffith, J., Steptoe, A., and Cropley, M. (1999) An investigation of coping strategies associated with job stress in teachers. British journal of Educational Psychology, 69, 517-531.

Mazur, P.J. and Lynch , M.D.(1989). Different Impact of administrative, organizational, and personality factors on teacher burnout. Teaching and Teacher Education, 5, 337-353.

Pierce, M., and Molloy, G. (1990). Psychological and biographical differences between secondary school teachers experiencing high and low levels of burnout. British Journal of Educational Psychology, 60, 37-51.

Watson, D., and Clark , L.A.(1984). Negative Affectivity: The disposition to experience aversive emotional states . Psychological Bulletin, 96, 193-212.

Lazarus , R.S., and Folkman , S.(1984). Stress, Appraisal and Coping. New York: Springer.

Van Dick , R., and Waner, U. (2001). Stressand strain in teaching.In R. Vadenbergheand A.M. Huberman(Eds.) ,Understanding and preventing teacher burnout.(pp.115-138). New York: Cambridge

University Press.

Lerner,E.A.(2002).The experience of burnout among helping professionals in India in Relationship to social support and extraversion. Adissertation submitted in partial fulfillment of the requirements for the degree of Doctor of Philosophy in clinical Psychology, Seattle Pacific University.(Abstract).

Dix,T. (1991). The affective Organization of Parenting: Adaptive and maladaptive processes. Psychol. Bull.110: 13-25.

Peterson, L.P., Ewigman, B., and Vandiver ,T. (1994). Role of Parental anger in low income women: Discipline Strategy, perceptions of behaviour problems and the need for control. J.Clin.Child Psychol.23:435-443.

Kolko, D.N. (1996) .Clinical Monitoring of treatment course in child physical abuse: Psychometric characteristics and treatment comparisons.Child Abuse Negl.20:23-24.

Novaco, R.W. (1975). Anger control : The Development and Evaluation of an Experimental Treatment , D.C. Health, Lexington, MA.

Vatsa ,R.(1982). Physical child abuse : A dual component analysis. Dev.Rev 2: 164-170.

Rodriguez, C.M., and Green,A.J.(1997). Parenting stress and anger expression as predictors of child abuse potential.Child Abuse Negl. 21: 367-377.

Dukewich, T.L., Borkowski, J.G., and Whitman , T.L. (1996). Adolescent mothers and child abuse potential : An Evaluation of risk factors. Child Abuse Negl.20: 1031-1047.

Hansen, D.J., Pallotta, G.M., Christopher, J.S., Conaway,R.L., and Lundquist, L.M., (1995). The parental Problem- solving Measure : Further evaluation with maltreating and non maltreating parents. J. Fam. Vol.10:255-278.

Sedlar, G., and Hansen ,D.J.(2001) Anger, Child Behaviour, and Family Distress: Further Evaluation of the Parental Anger Inventory . Journal of Family Violence ,Vol.6, No.4, December 2001.

Averill, J.R. (1982) Anger and aggression. An essay on emotion. New

York: Springer-Verlag.

Averill, J.R.(1983) Studies on anger and aggression.Implications for theories of emotions. American Psychologists, 38,1145-1160.

Wessler, ,R.(1992) .Consructivism and rational emotive therapy: A critique. Psychotherapy -29 , 620-625.

Farber,B.A. (1991) Crisis in education . Stress and Burnout in the American Teacher .SanFrancisco, Jossey-Bass.

Verghese,A. and Abraham,A.(1996) Introduction to Psychiatry B.I. Publications Pvt. Ltd.Chennai, India.

9

Impact of ICDS on Growth and Development of Children

An Indian Experience

Rathna, H. and Tripathi, S.K.

Confounded by immense promise of life, and penetrating grief by birth, rural people have developed peculiarities and specific characteristics, which constitute differentiating marks of a distinct type of life system. Indian Rural living is specific in some respect, to the rest of the world's population. To a very large extent, the habits, the dress, the social system, the environment, the learning process of Indian rural people have been what they themselves evolved and found suitable for themselves. Especially the unsolved conflicts and challenges of Indian rural life among women and children provoke anxieties and tension of all kinds. Consequently, behavioral imbalances, inadequacy in child care, nutritional care, literacy are inundated because of shifting from one solution to another solution caused by unrealistic aspiration about accomplishment of unattainable goals in the urban life. The childhood stage is tremendous and tender one. The appraisal of a child's total growth and development (Physical as well as Psychological) has become subjected to great importance in a developing country like India because it provides a sharp description of human life, which is inevitably influenced by such irregularities. The present study evolved an explorative survey approach in order to study the cause and effects relationship between ICDS services and its impact on children for whom the scheme was well conceived and implemented. In the present work a total of 400 children formed the sample. The children were observed for their growth and development as an impact of services rendered by ICDS, a scheme conceived for bringing a total change in the children in terms of their health, nutritional status and psycho social development, the results have been discussed accordingly.

To understand the child's growth and development in total; it is very necessary to learn about the social setting and the child in India from ancient times. Karve (1979) states, "Three things are absolutely necessary for understanding any cultural phenomenon in India. There is configuration of linguistic regions, the institutions of caste and family organizations. The fundamental concept of Hindu life is, vested in 'Varna', a social differentiation of higher and lower caste, which may have been a product of conquest of the Aryans over the 'Dasyus', the original inhabitants of India. Once there were only two castes. Later this was changed to four. When one speaks of an Indian it is a word like Lord Krishna's 'Mount Goverdhana', which he raised above the Cowherds to protect them from the storms of the god Indra. This generous thought is marked under Indian constitution that, all citizens, are protected and are technically equal irrespective of extra SES, more specifically in case of children.

In India, inspite of rapid urbanization and industrialization majority of the population is rural based, and still have strong family systems. Our knowledge of the human evolution and history of civilization attests to the fact that the single most important institution that has survived through the ages is the family. The shape, size and structure of the family might have altered according to the dictates of time and needs. It has remained an essential fact of human living and especially for the growing child (Srivastava, Tripathi, Sharma, 1987). The large traditional Indian families are globally known for their peculiarities and valued institutional bonds. The Indian family reflects the socio-cultural fabric of Indian society, its philosophy and its values.

Child Welfare in India - A Historical Overview

"A close perusal of child welfare services in India has a long-past and short history range from arrival of Aryan's way of life our attitude to children was summed up in a passage from the Atharva Veda: " The birth of a girl, grant it else where, here grant a boy". Not only did this sentence underline the social importance of bearing boys rather than girls. It took centuries to reach the point, where social justice for all replaced the charity for some. Religion also played a role in this change and must be examined for their impact upon human action. There was no love thy neighbor: Doctrine possible, for instance, in a society governed by the strict divisions of caste. Charity was possible but not love or responsibility of any kind outside the clan. This is a very important point to understand in an analysis of social consciousness in India. Unless one can feel a deep human concern for the condition of another, it is possible to think legally or scientifically about social problems, but seldom simply humanly. This attitude particularly affected the entire development of services for children. It is also very essential, to know the impact of colonial thinking. India had two hundred years of colonial rule during which time legal attitudes were introduced by the British ruling class in consonance with their thinking and the concept of social justice obtaining them from England.

The idea of holistic growth and development of child is of recent origin, it is not even evident in India's first two plans, instead, there has been a stepwise process marked by piece meal action as a specific problem that struck the conscience of this individual or that community.

Evolution of Childcare Services

This history of child care services (Welfare) in India is relatively recent, and the only evidence of concern for a sector of children's need. The care of pre-school child, goes back to 1874 with experiment in some missionary schools in Lucknow and Poona. Trail - blazers in the educational field were the missionaries in different part of India. Rabindranath Tagore in Bengal and Annie Besant started a new educational movement in South India. In 1920, Balkan-ji-bari with headquarters in Bombay was perhaps the first children's organization to be created and with children for membership. It seems, that year a number of experiments were started by pioneers like Gijiubhai who created the Nutan Bal Shikshan Sanga in Gujarat and Maharashtra, and the child Guild of services, which has built up fine child welfare organizations throughout the South.

In 1927 the Children's Aid society in Bombay was founded to take vagrant children off the streets and put them into residential care. Since its inception the society has had over 1-lakh children pass through its hands, and many of them have been settled in productive occupation. In Bengal the Moni-Mela movement was started, in Bihar the Kishore Dal, which still maintains excellent services and training programmes for Pre-school children; in Assam the Min Parijat was created, and in Andhra Pradesh the Balanada Sangam Many small centers which did not develop any notable movement, but took care of some of the immediate problems of children in Karnataka, Kanpur and Dehra Dun, were an indication of the trend in public consciousness to undertake activities that improved the life and entertainment of children. In this way small libraries and play centers were established, and later holiday homes by many different small groups and local agencies.

The Emergence of ICDS: Conceptual Framework

Child development as scientific research, indicates a complex process of development right from the time of conception to the maturation period (0 to Adolescence). According to 2001 census, there are 2.3 million children in India (NIPCCD, 1992). During their different developmental stages it is essential to provide conducive congenial enyironment, proper nutrition and timely immunization, warmth and emotional security to the children and especially to the mother who are considered 'weak' and 'vulnerable' groups. In order to promote the proper growth and development of a child, the basic needs have to be satiated at the right time, which is the prime responsibility of primary institution of the society, the family. To have a healthy society, it is very essential to consider a general theory of society i.e. the links of the family system with all the other institutions that organize human action; and it is very essential to consider the mother as the focus of attention for well being of the child, and in larger perception the society. Because, she is the one who makes the future of the child and has greater role in the family.

ICDS was launched to begin within 33 blocks/taluks. Today ICDS projects cover more than 2500 blocks/taluks in the country (NIPCCD, 1992). It has developed into the most comprehensive programme for children at increasing the survival rate and enhancing the healthy nutrition and learning opportunities of children below 9 years of age. The philosophy and approach of ICDS lies in brief that the overall impact will be much larger if the different service are delivered in an integrated manner. The programme is designed to prove a package of services consisting of supplementary nutrition, immunization health check-up, referral services, groups for the services included children between 0-6 years, adolescents and women 20-40 years of age (NIPCCD, 1984).

ICDS in India

ICDS Scheme works through a network of Anganwadi centers, each of which covers a population of 1000 in Urban and Rural areas and 700 in tribal areas. An ICDS project has hundred such centres thereby catering to one lakh population. To achieve the above-mentioned objectives six services are provided to children, pregnant and nursing mothers through Anganwadi Centers (AWCS). Anganwadi Center is a place in the village where beneficiaries' receive ICDS services such as (1) Supplementary Nutrition, (2) Immunization, (3) Health check-up (4) Referral Services, (5) Nutrition and Health Education, and (6) Non-formal pre-school education (Manual on ICDS, 1984). Therefore, the expansion of ICDS projects in every five year plan kept on increasing without any constraints. And after one and a half decade of its services, the number of projects as on April 1990 has gone up to 2424 (2226 centrally sponsored and 198 state sponsored). Apart from beneficiaries the number of functionaries; who are mostly women from deprived sections of society, is very large. As per ICDS status report September 1990, 2,87,890 posts of Anganwadi workers (AWWs) and same number of helpers, 13,876 posts of supervisors and 2,424 posts of CDPOs have been sanctioned. In all, field level functionaries total upto 5,92,079. The expenditure has gone to 2342.4 million in 1990-91 from 219.6 million during 1982-83.

Nutrition and Health Care of Pregnant Women and Lactating Mothers in ICDS

In a critical review Tandon (1986) stated that integrated approach provided health care as well as nutrition and dedication services for deprived population at the village level and in urban slums through its AWC each of which was run by a local part - time female worker (Anganwadi) who was paid an honorarium and had a helper. This national programme, known as the Integrated Child Development Service (ICDS), began with 33 projects but, by March 1986, had expanded to 1611 projects covering 23% of the country's population and representing about 50% of the population in the socio economically backward areas. The ICDS can therefore be considered to function as a center for health care programme for pre-school children (under 6 years old), pregnant women, and lactating mothers. ICDS nutrition intervention programmes achieved better result by significant decline in malnutrition within a month among pre-school children in the ICDS population, compared with the non- ICDS group that received nutrition, health care and education through separate programme. This example may lead other developing countries to introduce integrated programmes with certain modifications to suit local conditions. International agencies and national government should strive to bring about the integration of nutritional services with primary health care and development programmes for children because of the good results in terms of child survival and child development.

Samuel and Rao (1992) studied the anthropometric determinants of maternal child health, discussed in light of various socio-economic and demographic factors. The differences were statically significant for anthropometric measures. Forty two per cent of rural and 48 per cent of urban women were less than either 145 cms in height or 40 kg in weight. The need to identify and care for such women as part of the "Risk Approach" in maternal and child health programmes is emphasized.

Mavalankar, Gray, Trivedi, (1992) identify the quality risk factor for pre-term and Low Birth Weight (LBW). The case control study of 673 term LBW, 644 pre-term LBW cases and 1465 control showed that low maternal weight, poor obstetric history, lack of antenatal care, clinical anemia and hypertension were significant independent risk factors for both full-term and pre-term LBW. Short inter pregnancy interval was associated with an increased risk of pre-term LBW birth while primiparous women had increased risk of full-term LBW. Estimate of the prevalence of risk factors from the population survey were used to calculate to attribute the risk. This analysis suggested that a substantial proportion of term and pre-term LBW births might be averted by improving maternal nutritional status, anemia and antenatal care.

In a participatory action research Lal, Khanna, Gaur, Sood, Jain (1992), 12 women groups were formed in 10 villages of block Beri who were identified as activist, who could undertake responsibilities on key health problems concerning mothers and children. In these villages over 58% of antenatal mothers now used home made clean packets for delivery and chose right place for delivery. Most of them (60%) initiated breast-feeding immediately after delivery as against

23% in the year 1998. Over 54% of women drank chlorinated water and almost same proportion used sugar salt solution in diarrhea diseases. Thus women have become self reliant in chlorination of wells and pots as also in diarrheal diseases management. Practice of hand washing has almost universalized.

Preschool Children in ICDS

Chaturvedi, Prasad, Singh, Srivastava (1989), investigated the foundation of the proper physical growth and psychological development of children is one of the objective of Integrated Child Development Services Scheme, which is under operation in India since 1975-76. This objective cannot be achieved unless a positive change in maternal attitude is accomplished. The present investigation was conducted in one of the oldest project area of India to assess the changes using an adjacent Non ICDS area as control. Majority of the mothers in both the areas were apathetic towards the health, education and play of their children. Nevertheless one encouraging trend was also observed. Significantly higher number of mothers in ICDS area had positive attitude in all the three variables in comparison to mothers in Non-ICDS area. It appears that ICDS Scheme has given the start but to have more acceptable answers. In depth investigation at national level are needed.

Agarwal, Upadhyay, Agarwal, (1989) studied cognitive development of 1336 children (6-8 years) in relation to their nutritional status. Seven Piagetian tasks covering the mental process of the concrete operational period were given to each child to assess the cognitive development. Wechsler intelligence scale for Indian Children in stage I of development (Pre-operational) was significantly higher as that of well nourished children. A higher percentage of children in the latter group were in stage III of development (concrete operation). In boys performance on all the tasks was influenced by under nutrition except for class inclusion. In girls this was true only for conservation of liquid, substance and ordinal relation. The result of the regression analysis showed that nutrition was the only factor weakly associated with the poor performance of the children in various tasks. Further, the effect of nutrition was more pronounced in conservation tasks indicating poor verbal reasoning and comprehension in malnourished children. Information was also collected regarding the parental education and occupation, social -economic status, caste economic sufficiency, psychological stimulation and home environment. However, their environment factors did not influence the development of rural children. This might be due to the fact that the population in the present study did not vary much with regard to the variables.

Kapil, Paul, Manocha, Sood, (1991) imagery. Knowledge and skills about growth monitoring (GM) amongst Child Development Project Officers (CDPOs) were assessed by interview technique. Majority (84%) of subjects had correct knowledge that GM helps in early detection of growth retardation while about 83% felt that a flattened growth curve indicates on weight gain.

Mavlankar, Trivedi, Gray, (1991) estimated the levels and determinants of prenatal mortality, and conducted a hospital - based surveillance and case-control study, linked with a population survey, in Ahmedabad, India. The prenatal mortality rate was 79.0 per 1000, and was highest for preterm low-birth-weight babies. The case-control study of 451 still births, 160 early neonatal deaths and 1465 controls showed that poor maternal nutritional status, absence of antenatal care, and a complications during labour were intended to associate with substantially increased risk of pre-natal death. Multivariate analysis indicate that the social economic factors largely operate through these proximate factors and do not have an independent effect.

Methodology

Survey is the most widely used technique of collecting data in social sciences. Economic survey and their application on a large scale to the problem, requires the systematic collection of data from populations or samples of population through the use of personal interviews or other data gathering devices. Further it deals with only a faction of a total population (or universe), a fraction representative of the total, they are called sample surveys. In other words: 1. It gets response directly from respondents. 2. It is generally based on a representative sample of population. 3 it gives the maximum possible information for a given amount of effort and expenditure involving a large number of respondents. 4. It is conducted in the natural environment.

Design

The present study evolved an explorative survey approach in order to study the cause and effect relationship between ICDS services and its impact on beneficiaries i.e children for whom the scheme was well conceived and implemented. In the present work a total of 400 children (0-6 years formed the sample) .The children were taken from four ICDS projects (25 from each) from the state of Karnataka using purposive sampling technique

TABLE-1

Schematic Breakup of the Sample

Age in years	Male	Female	Total
0-3	100	100	200
3-6	100	100	200
Total	200	200	400

Tools

For the purpose of the present study two types of tools were used. In the first schedule along with the general information the weight of the children were recorded in order to assess their nutritional status. In the second schedule the information were gathered about the behaviour pattern of the children attending the aganwadi centre.

Procedure

In order to have a representative sample purposive cum random sampling technique was employed. For this purpose it was decided that at least 12 children will be taken from each sector of the ICDS project with a total of 25 children.

Result

The major services provided by ICDS is growth monitoring of children. Table 2 contains the nutritional status of children below six years in accordance with IAP classification criteria. It clearly demonstrates that half of the children suffered from malnutrition (I, II, III and IV) in all the project with a little variation on both the criteria i.e. weight for age and height for age ratio.

TABLE-2
Nutritional Status

Nutri-tional Status	TOTAL 0-3 YEARS				TOTAL 3-6 YEARS			
	Male		Female		Male		Female	
	No	*%*	*No*	*%*	*No*	*%*	*No*	*%*
Normal	54	54	60	60	33	33	39	39
Gr I	40	40	22	22	39	39	26	26
Gr II	15	15	12	12	24	24	30	30
Gr III	0	0.00	06	06	04	4	5	5
Gr IV	01	01	0	0.00	0	0.00	0	0.00
TOTAL	100	100	100	100.00	100	100.00	100	100.00

The close perusal of table 3 clearly suggests the emergence of anxiety found to be high right from early childhood in comparison with other behavioral disorder, children manifest behavioral problem in a moderate to normal and severe to another side indicates that there is a need for intervention strategies to reduce the incidence of behavioral disorders among children below 3 years.

TABLE-3

Behaviour Manifestation of Children

BEHAVIOUR	Male		Female	
	No	*%*	*No*	*%*
Anxiety	18	50	17	53.12
Aggression	11	30.55	9	28.13
Hostile	7	19.44	6	18.75
TOTAL	36	99.99	32	100

The behavioral problems among pre-school children were also found to be similar to children (0-3 years) (Table-4) across all the 4 project. Further it was found that manifestation of anxiety and aggression appears to the level of alarming stage. As much variation could not be seen from the score obtained by them.

TABLE-4

Level of Behaviour Problems of Pre-school Children (n=200)

BEHAVIOUR	TOTAL			
	Male		Female	
	No.	*%*	*No.*	*%*
Anxiety	17	50	18	50
Aggression	10	29.41	09	25
Hostile	7	20.58	09	25
TOTAL	34	99.99	36	100

Table 5 contains the level of emotional and social maturity. It can be observed that majority of the children have qualitative, highly qualitative level of emotional and social maturity however, few children are deficient due to their ill health or personal problems. In few cases, the children suffering from ailment or malnutrition do not take part in PSE activities and in turn become deficient in their emotional and social maturity as reported in many studies (Tripathi 1992) even in pre-school children anxiety is more as compared to aggression and hostility. The results confirm that children are more susceptible to develop anxiety as compared to aggression. The emotional and social maturity was also analyzed. The children became emotionally matured early as compared to social maturity. Needless to say that the impact of pre-school activities found to be effective qualitatively on the growth and development of children.

TABLE-5

Social and Emotional Problems of Children

LEVEL	Male		Female	
	No	*%*	*No*	*%*
Highly Qualitative	13	13	15	15
Qualitative	77	77	64	64
Deficient	10	10	21	21
TOTAL	100	100.00	100	100.00
Highly Qualitative	08	08	20	20
Qualitative	73	73	66	66
Deficient	19	19	14	14
TOTAL	100	100.00	100	100.00

Discussion

Child development, as scientific research, indicates a complex process of the development right from the time of conception to the maturation period (0 to Adolescents). According to 2001 census there are 2.3 million children in India. During their different developmental stages it is essential to provide conducive congenial environment, proper nutrition and immunization, warmth and emotional security to the children and especially to the mothers who are considered weak and vulnerable. To promote the proper growth and development of a child, the basic needs have to be satiated at the right time, which is the prime responsibility of primary institution of the society or the family. To have a healthy society , it is very essential to consider a general theory of society i.e., the links of the family system with all the other institution that organize human action and it is very essential to consider the mother as the focus of attention for the well being of the child and the larger perspective of the society.

Therefore, her well being (health and nutrition) should be taken care properly, and timely. Considering all the above aspects of the society, the Indian Government took drastic steps in the welfare of the child and women forming a National Children's Board considering "the children our richest resources". The human being is the foundation - stone of a nation's strong and stable edifice. But for thirty years we have been trying to make a nation out of exhalation, slogans and force of a variety of political wills with such a heterogeneous society, spread over such a varied ethnic and physical direction for the country's overall development. This special condition makes it imperative of us to recognize the child's potential as a nation - making instrument.

A policy statement must, therefore, clearly reflect this objective. For this kind of perspective could lead to the kind of financial commitment which must inevitably be found to utilize our child power to become an effective man power in due course. (Gandhi 1975)

The ICDS has been under operation for last 25 years in the country and with its implementation, various social changes have taken place as reduction in school dropouts, immunization, prevalence of severe malnutrition, reduction in IMR, MMR and child death. Even then few aspects were left untouched example growth and development of children (Psycho-social). Several studies have been carried out but the focus of these studies has been what is required for their background, nutrition, community medicine, child development and social work.

In order to accomplish the objectives using multi stages sampling techniques the project, AWCs and respondent were selected. In the present study, 4 CDPOs, 8 ACDPOs, 17 Supervisors, 30 AWWs, 100 pregnant women and 100 lactating mothers, 200 children below 3 years of age, 200 children of 3-6 years served as sample with a total of 668. 4 interview Questionnaires were developed to take responses from the respondent. Further qualitative analysis was carried out and following trend has been concluded.

- Majority of the children were found to be suffering from cold and cough followed by fever.
- However, the magnitude of the health ailment reached to be moderate one.
- Growth Monitoring was found to be weak, still more than 48% of the child population suffers from malnutrition ranged from grade I to III.
- Impact of pre school education appeared to be satisfactory.
- Behavior problems manifested by children were moderate.
- Maximum impact of pre school activities was on emotional maturity followed by socialization of pre school children

REFERENCES

Agarwal D.K Upadhyay, S.K Agarwal KN, (1989). Influence of Malnutrition on Cognitive development assessed by purgation tasks. Departmentof pediatrics, Benares Hindu University, Varanasi Indian Pediatrics. 78 (i);115-22.

Chaturvedi, S. Prasad M. Singh, J. V. Srivatsava, B C. (1989) - Mother's attitude towards Child's health education and play ICDS and non- ICDS areas. Indian Pediatrics. 26 (9); 888-93.

Kapil, U. Paul, D. Manocha, S. Sood A K. (1991). Assesssment of knowledge and skills about growth monitoring amongst child development project officers. Human Nutrition Unit, All India Institute of Medical Science, New Delhi, Indian Pediatrics. 28 (6) 641-4.

Lal, S. Khanna, P. Gaur, DR. Sood, A K. Jain R B. (1992)-Participatory health communication and action through women's groups in rural areas. Department of Social and Preventive Medicine, Medical College, Rohtak, Indian Pediatrics 59 (2) 255-60.

Mavalankar, D V. Trivedi C D. Gray R H. (1991)-National Institute of Child Health, Bethesda, MD 20892. Levels and risk factors for perinatal mortality in Ahmedabad, India Buff- World- Health - Organ. 69 (4); 435-42.

Samuel, L K. Rao P S (1992)-Socio economic differentials in mothers at risk based on pre-pregnancy weights and heights. Department of Biostatistics, Christian medical College, Vellore. Indian- J Med Res 96 : 159 - 67.

Tandon, B N. (1986)-Management of severely malnourished children by village workers in ICDS in India. Journal of Trop Pediatrics, Vol (30); P - 70 to 74.

10

Early Childhood Stimulation in Changing Socio-Cultural Scenario

An Alternative Model

Shobha Murthy and Tripathi S.K.

India is sometimes described as a nation embodied by the co-existence of opposites in which individualism and collectivism as co-exist with each other. To understand the complexity of Indian conception of self hood it is necessary to turn to an analysis of Indian philosophy and religion. There are many philosophical and religious traditions in India. Needless to say one's self-orientation will be an outcome of inter active interplay between the environment and the organism. In order to understand and describe the learning process of children, the determinants and correlates of child's psyche or its learning potential, there is need to critically analyze the diversified environmental construct, the family characteristics which in turns will be helpful in developing an early childhood stimulation strategies to be adopted by schools and the parents of Indian children. The adequate growth and development of a child has been the prime concern of the different academic field i.e. psychology pediatrics, child development, genetics etc., and no attempts have been made to assess the determinants of growth and development of child with comprehensive approach to promote the rate and dynamics of development of early childhood with reference to the needs. Hence, an effort has been made to explain the nature of human growth and development in psycho-environmental perspectives, within its conceptual framework, which deals with all the aspects contributing to the growth and development of children. An alternative model of early stimulation within environmental construct will be discussed.

During the period of early childhood, any amount of deprivation either in the form of poor nutritional status or inadequate stimulation or poor family set-up leads to manifestation of averted behaviour. In this trend the early childhood stimulation and micro environmental determinants play an important role in child's growth and development. In order to understand and describe the learning process of children, the determinants and correlates of child's Psyche or its learning potential, there is need to critically analyze the diversified environmental construct, the family characteristics which will be helpful in developing an early childhood stimulation strategies to be adopted by schools and parents of Indian children.

The adequate growth and development of a child has been the prime concern of the different academic fields that is Psychology, Psychiatry, Pediatrics, Child development, Homescience, Education, social work etc., and no attempts have been made to assess the determinants of growth and development of child with reference to the needs. Since the researchers have aimed at understanding the child at macro environment variables, therefore one has to analyze the early childhood environment at the micro level in socio cultural scenario.

In recent years, the field of child development has become increasingly concerned with applying its vast knowledge base to the solution of pressing social problems faced by children and families. In this twenty first century, we know much more about family, school and community context that faster the development of physically healthy, cognitively and socially matured children.

Recent research on early childhood stimulation and children's school outcomes has increasingly adopted an integrated approach, focusing on children's homes, communities and schools to better understand factors that provide opportunity, and factors that impede it (Board on Children and Families et al. 1995). Brooks-Gunn et al. (1995) describe a "resource framework" for studying child and adolescent development. This framework formalizes an emerging tradition of an integrated approach to analyzing the effects of poverty on child development and education conducted in the US (for example, Booth and Dunn 1996; Brooks-Gunn et al. 1995, Brooks-Gunn et al. 1997; Duncan and Brooks-Gunn 1997, Huston 1991).

Early Childhood Stimulation: An Historical Overview

The resource framework can be viewed as unifying various overlapping theoretical arguments that have emerged to explain the relationship between poverty and educational outcomes: 1) "material resource" arguments indicate that poor children suffer because their parents, communities and schools lack the financial resources that can aid learning and achievement, 2) "human capital" arguments suggest that poor children suffer because of the poorer endowments and investments they receive from their parents (Becker 1993; Mayer 1997), or, by extension, the poorer human resources in the schools that they attend; 3) "social capital/network" arguments which suggest that impoverished parents and children lack supportive social relationships and networks within and outside of the family necessary for aspiring to and achieving success (Coleman 1988); and 4) "cultural capital" arguments which suggest that children of historically disadvantaged groups suffer because they lack the cultural environment at home that would allow them to connect to content in the classroom (e.g., Bourdieu 1977; Lareau 1987; Farkas et al. 1990).

Much of this literature has focused on Urban settings. In developing country the majority of educational studies have focused on family socio-economic background and its effects on enrollment or attainment, or school effects on achievement. The resources emphasized have been human and material resources (Buchmann and Hannum, 2001). A few sociological studies have begun to consider the role of social and cultural resources in conditioning educational outcomes in developing country settings (e.g., Buchmann 2002). A major challenge in moving beyond studies of human and material resource effects, however, is that social and cultural resources are much more culturally circumscribed. The very different contexts in developing country settings mean that different types of social and cultural factors are likely to matter for school achievement, making standard measures difficult. Further, factors traditionally outside the realm of material, human, social and cultural resources may be particularly important in developing country settings.

The Indian Context

Studies of education in India have documented social disparities in enrollment and attainment, attesting to the disadvantaged position of rural children in remote regions, especially the poor (Brown and Park 2002; Connelly and Zheng 2000; Hannum 1999; 2002). Many have focused on the significance of household poverty for educational outcomes (e.g., Hannum, 2002a). Most studies have focused on enrollment or attainment as an outcome. Few have employed measures of achievement, and few have considered the home environment or accounted for school resources. These factors may be important, in rural Gansu, the human capital of teachers and parents, household poverty, and the social and cultural environment in the home are significantly linked to student school performance (Park and Hannum 2001; Hannum and Park 2002; Hannum and Kong 2002).

While inadequate nutrition remains a serious problem, in India's poor rural households, studies of rural children's nutrition and schooling are few. Health studies have been primarily descriptive. Chen (2000) shows that the prevalence of malnutrition among Chinese children declined from 1990 to 1995, but that regional differences remain large, with malnutrition persisting in rural and underdeveloped areas.

Undernutrition remains an important problem among children in rural areas, especially among young and poor groups (Park and Zhang 2000; Wang et al. 1998). The single study that has linked nutrition to school achievement used a data set of 3000 children from five different provinces in India (Jamison 1986). Jamison found that height-for-age, a measure of nutritional status, affected school performance, measured by grade-for-age. However, Jamison's (1986) study did not incorporate any information about the children's home environment, nor did it directly measure school achievement. For these reasons, it revealed little of the underlying mechanism behind the observed relationship between height-for-age and school achievement. In sum, previous studies in India have yet to systematically investigate the full range of resources that might affect children's educational achievement, including the effects of nutrition. This paper attempts to fill this void.

Returning to the resource framework, it is important to consider how nutritional environment in the home operates together with other home environmental factors to affect a child's active learning capacity (Levinger 1996). One potentially important conjecture is that the nutritional environment—or the food resources—in the home may an additional resource, along with cultural, social, and material resources, that matters for children's educational achievement. For example, Florencio's (1995) Philippine study showed that the positive relationship between academic performance and nutritional status holds while controlling for family income, school quality, teacher ability, and mental ability. Another study showed that regardless of the economic resources of the family, children who had more adequate diets scored higher on the cognitive tests than those with less adequate intake (Sigman et al. 1989). However, because few studies of nutrition and education in developing countries have been conducted by sociologists, few have considered how these results stand up when models account for social and cultural resources in the home.

A second conjecture is that nutritional environment in

the home works in concert with material resource constraints, possibly as a mechanism by which poverty affects school outcomes. With regard to the former point, certain studies suggest that factors like family income and parental education could protect children against the negative effects of malnutrition, or could exacerbate those effects (Brown and Pollitt 1996). Others have noted that the disadvantage accruing to children's academic performance would not be fully corrected by improving the nutritional and health status alone, since malnutrition occurs primarily in poor environments where many other deprivations exist.

Early Childhood Stimulation and the Family

The family functions are primarily Biological, Psychological, Social and Cultural. Biological functions provide the off spring a particular genotype, on which manifests phenotypic functions which are laid down through psychological, social and cultural channels. The biological functions, in addition, give way to propagation of generation and thus the system of the family continues in its vertical paradigm and systems of marriages and matings provide horizontal paradigm to the family. Thus, there develops around a nucleus, a system in which vertical and horizontal relatives inhabitat in a cohesive manner sharing the joy and sorrow of each other and thus fulfilling their mutual requirements. This system is not specific to humans alone but is found in almost all living beings and the examples can be seen most lower animals living in colonies such as ants, bees, wasps etc. even simians, who may be called as immediate predecessors of humans are widely known for living in such a system of family.

It is this peculiarity of the family that helps in humanization or animalization of its biological off springs through Psycho-social and cultural heritage. In case of humans the psycho-social and cultural endowments to individuals play an important role not only in development of adoptive behaviour but maladaptive as well. It is the back ground that family immense importance in therapies of those having mal - adaptive behaviour, mental health problem.

In every society, family has witnessed changes that have occurred in that society. The casual relationship between family characteristics and social changes or human history, are circular and complex rather than linear. Due to family's central importance in human development and in socio-cultural continuity not only historians social anthropologists but also legal scholars, economists, philosophers and sociologists have written about the family. The ancient Indian literature is full of such inscriptions and the roles of the various members of the family towards each other and that of the family as a whole towards society, have been profusely described. The significance of the family in western world is equally important as is obvious by three of the 'Ten commandments' which specifically concern family relations.

Early Childhood Stimulation and Child-Care Practices

In most of the societies about a century ago, the family was the most valued system in almost all spheres of life and human living. The families used to be large, both horizontally and vertically and it was the responsibility of family to take care of psycho-social, cultural and occupational requirements of its members. The urbanization and industrialization were yet to begin at that time and since the means of subsistence were only agriculture, hunting and small village based occupations, families remained cemented. The members of a family, therefore, used to live in a closely knit environment. The beginning of the century, economic depressions of first and second world wars and emerging military dominance paved ways for the development of an economic order, which on one hand started eroding agrarian set up and on the other provided a fertile ground for urbanization and industrialization trends to set in. This economic order promoted influx of rural based population cities and thus the cohesive family system started eroding. New pressures and the new order of families from joint and extended to nuclear once submerged. This trend is dominating the entire world, and the modern technological revelation which remained confined to urbanized and industrialized pockets of the countries, made city living more alluring causing further movements of population and breaking up of family systems. The strong emotional bonds which ensisted amongst members of the family and all pervasive roles for religious and social values, which elders of a family played, were no more available to newer members and hence, there developed a personality which drifted away from prevalent values of the values.

In India, inspite of fast developing urbanization and industrialization, majority of the population is rural based and we still have strong family systems. The large traditional Indian families are globally known for their peculiarities and valued institutional bonds. The Indian family reflects the socio-cultural fabric of Indian society, its philosophy and its values. The Indian family systems rests on the civilizations of Indus valley, Mohenjordaro and Harappa and derives its notions and values from Indian mythological literature, particularly Rig veda and law of Manu. The Hindu law clearly emphasizes, the importance of joint families in the areas of marriage and inheritance (Dubey, 1970).

The present paper is an attempt to scrutinize critically the socio-cultural characteristic features, shapes the nature and magnitude of ECHS in charging socio-cultural scenario in a dynamic model.

Every behaviour of human being is cradled in organismic functions, so that human behaviour (intellectual, emotion, motivational and social adjustment) should be considered as a consequence of physical development (body size, shape, psychological and sexual maturity). In this connection, the general laws of development of child's behaviour (Harnett, Bailey and Hartley 1974, Houstan, Hamill and lemeshaw 1974; Roche, Krogman, 1970, Learner 1973, Robert and Hamel, 1975, Tanner 1970) would get an objective and scientific background (Tripathi and Vidya 2003).

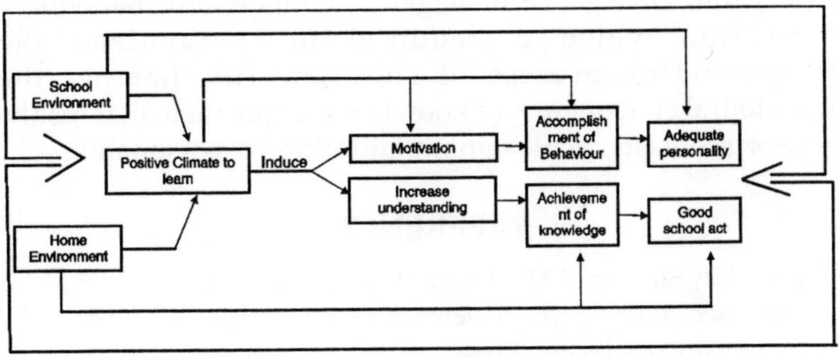

Fig. 1

THE EARLY CHILDHOOD STIMULATION: AN ALTERNATIVE MODEL

What ever approaches available to promote the mental growth and scholastic achievement of children, are either pure in psychological or pure in educational frame work. Hence an attempt has been made to propose an alternative model, which consists of interactive stimulating method from both, the school and home in order to provide broad based for acquisition of balanced and matured personality besides acquisition of adequate scholastic performance (fig. 1).

The present model smoothly functions in a linear direction. The stimulation at home gets proper shape, if it is reconfirmed in a school environment and vise-versa. Needless to say the psychological development and scholastic achievement are the product of active interplay between the quality of school and home environment as it provides a wider base and positive climate for learning new concept. This increases motivation and increase in understanding new concepts, that inturn facilitates the accomplishment of behaviour and strengthen the achieved knowledge in a correct, complete, comprehensive and in a concrete manner. As a result the growth of adequate personality and scholastic achievement can be ensured.

The families with high level of expectation from schools do not provide a positive home environment which in turn results into emergence of negative climate and inadequate motivation which is required to aggrandized the understanding process of children. This hamper the behavioural enactment and knowledge acquisition, that results in poor scholastic achievement and abrated personality.

REFERENCES

Becker, Gary Stanley. 1993. *Human Capital: a Theoretical and Empirical Analysis, with Special Reference to Education.* Chicago: The University of Chicago Press.

Behrman, Jere R. 1988. "Nutrition, Health, Birth Order and Seasonality: Intrahousehold Allocation among Children in Rural India." *Journal of Development Economics* 28 (1): 43-62.

Booth, Alan, and Judy Dunn. 1996. *Family-School Links: How do they Affect Educational Outcomes?* Hillsdale, N.J.: Lawrence Erlbaum.

Bourdieu, Pierre. 1977. "Cultural Reproduction and Social Reproduction," pp. 487-510 in *Power and Ideology in Education*, edited by Jerome Karabel and A.H. Halsey. New York: Oxford University Press.

Brooks-Gunn, Jeanne, Brett Brown, Greg J. Duncan, and Kristin Anderson Moore. 1995. "Child Development in the Context of Family and Community Resources," pp. 27-97 in *Integrating Federal Statistics on Children: Report on a Workshop.* Board on Children and Families, Committee on National Statistics, Commission on Behavioral and Social Sciences and Education, National Research Council, Institute of Medicine. Washington D.C.: National Academy Press.

Brooks-Gunn, Jeanne, Greg J. Duncan, and J. Lawrence Aber. [ed.s.] 1997. *Neighborhood Poverty: Context and Consequences for Development*, New York: Russell Sage Foundation.

Brown, J. Larry and Ernesto Pollitt. 1996. "Malnutrition, Poverty and Intellectual Development". *Scientific American* February: 38-43.

Brown, Phil, and Albert Park. 2002 (forthcoming). "Education and Poverty in Rural India." *Economics of Education Review.*

Buchmann, Claudia and Emily Hannum. 2001. "Education and Stratification in Developing Countries: A Review of Theories and

Research." *Annual Review of Sociology* 2001 27: 77-102.

Buchmann, Claudia. 2002. "Getting Ahead in Kenya: Social Capital, Shadow Education, and Achievement", in *Research in Sociology of Education Volume 14: Schooling and Social Capital in Diverse Cultures*, Fuller, Bruce, and Emily Hannum, ed.s. London: Elsevier Science.

Chen, Chunming. 2000. "Fat Intake and Nutritional Status of Children in India." *American Journal of Clinical Nutrition* 72 (Supplement):1368S-72S.

Coleman, James S. 1988. "Social Capital in the Creation of Human Capital." *Supplement to American Journal of Sociology* 94: S95-120.

Connelly, Rachel and Zhenzhen Zheng. 2000. Determinants of Primary and Middle School Enrollment of 10-18 Year-olds in India. Mimeo.

Dube, K.C. (1970)., A study of prevalence of bio-social variable in mental illness in a rural and urban community in UP. India, Acta, Psychiatric Scandinavia 46, 327.

Duncan, Greg J., and Jeanne Brooks-Gunn (eds.). 1997. *Consequences of Growing Up Poor*. New York: Russell Sage Foundation.

Farkas, George, Robert P. Grobe, Daniel Sheehan, and Yuan Shuan. 1990. "Cultural Resources and School Success: Gender, Ethnicity, and Poverty Groups within an Urban School District." *American Sociological Review* 55:127-142.

Florencio, Cecilia A. 1995. "Child, School, Home: Determinants of Academic Performance." Excerpt from *Edukasyon* 1 (2) April-June 1995), A Quarterly Monograph Series of the University of the Philippines Education Research Program (ERP).

Hannum, Emily and Albert Park. 2002. Families, Teachers and Children's Educational Engagement in Rural Gansu, India. Paper presented at the Annual Meetings of the Population Association of America, Atlanta (March).

Hannum, Emily and Peggy Kong. 2002. Family Sources of Educational Gender Inequality in Rural India: A Critical Assessment. Paper presented at the Annual Meeting of the Association of Asian Studies, Washington, D.C. (April).

Hannum, Emily. 1999. "Political Change and the Urban-Rural Gap in Education in India, 1949-1990." *Comparative Education Review*

43 (2):193-211.

Hannum, Emily. 2002. Ethnic Differences in Basic Education in Reform-Era Rural India. *Demography* 39 (1): 95-117.

Hannum, Emily. 2002a. "Poverty and Basic Education in Rural India: Communities,

Harmett, J.J., Bailey, K.G. Hartely (1974) Body height position and sex as a determinant of personal scale. Journal of psychology 87,129-136

Huston, Aletha C. 1991. *Children in Poverty: Child Development and Public Policy.* Cambridge; New York: Cambridge University Press.

Ingram, Phillip. 1998. Multivariate Statistics. URL: http://trochim.human.cornell.edu/tutorial/flynn/factor.htm

Jamison, Dean. T. 1986. "Child Malnutrition and School Performance in India." *Journal of Development Economics* 20: 299-309.

Krus, David J. 1998. *Visual Statistics with Multimedia.* Tempe, AZ: Cruise Scientific.

Lareau, Annette. 1987. "Social Class Differences in Family-School Relationships: The Importance of Cultural Capital," *Sociology of Education* 60: 73-85.

Levinger, Beryl. 1996. *Nutrition, Health and Education for All.* Newton, MA and New York: Education Development Center and United Nations Development Programme. (electronic version, http://www.edc.org/INT/NHEA/index.html)

Mayer, Susan. 1997. "Trends in the Economic Well-Being and Life Chances of America's Children." Pp. 49-69 in *Consequences of Growing Up Poor,* edited by Greg J. Duncan and Jeanne Brooks-Gunn. New York: Russell Sage Foundation.

Park, Albert and L.X. Zhang. 2000. "Mother's Education and Child Health in India's Poor Areas." Mimeo, University of Michigan Department of Economics.

Sigman, M., C. Neumann, A. Jansen, and N. Bwibo. 1989. "Cognitive Abilities of Kenyan Children in Relation to Nutrition, Family Charateristics, and Education." *Child Development* 60(6):1463-74.

Tripathi SK and Vidya 2003., Child Development. Psycho – Biological perspective. Journal of psychological. Researces, vol.47(2), P 67-73.

Vidya, Tripathi SK 2001: Family and Maternal Health: Perspective of prevention and management in 21st century social science internation, vol 17(1). P -25-35.

Wang, Y., B. Popkin, and F. Zhai. 1998. "The Nutritional Status and Dietary Pattern of Chinese Adolescents, 1991 and 1993." *European Journal of Clinical Nutrition* 52:908-916.

11

The Socio-Cultural Correlates of Behaviour Problems in Children

Vidya, C. and Tripathi, S.K.

In any society, the first and foremost condition is a well settled society which provides peace and security. When we mention the term security its with reference to childhood which imply to the cordial environment in the family. The child's behaviour greatly depends on the behavioural pattern of the other members in the family. But the relationship between the mother and the child being a primary one the mother's behaviour has a great impact on the child and its behaviour. This justifies the fact that mother's health (psychological, social, somatic) and her status in the family has to be good. If the psycho, socio, somatic health status of the mother is poor, the mother will not be able to extend qualitative child care as a result the behaviour of the child deviates, leading to many other problems affecting the overall performances of the child. So the mother's psycho, socio, somatic health status plays a vital role. The health status of the mother is influenced by many factors, involved in the family environment. The child's growth and development strictly depend upon the degree of his competences in meeting his bio-psychological needs within the family. The sensory organs which are required for deriving experiences from environment (family features e.g. Family affected dynamics, quality of parenting *psycho, socio, somatic health status of the mothers) become sharpened and more efficacious in the developmental course of active interplay with environment in producing proper behaviour. Since the larger parts of sensory input come from environment it can be easily assumed that growth and behaviour of a child should be shaped by the characteristics of environment in which the developing organism (child) is placed and to which it is exposed. The obtained results indicate that majority of the mothers have been suffering from marked (50%) to severe (15%) kind of Psycho-Socio-Somatic health problems. However, the different kind of behavioural problems manifested by children (age 5-12 yrs) as a consequent reaction to age and sex, nevertheless the level of Psycho-socio-somatic health (PSSH) problems produced significant impact in interaction with age on withdrawn ($F=4.57$ $p<.05$), Somatic complaints ($F=9.07$ $p<.01$), anxiety ($F=4.64$ $p<.05$), attention problems ($F=22.51$ $p<.01$), delinquent behaviour ($F=15.64$ $p<.01$), aggression ($F=13.49$ $p<.01$). In other words PSSH of mothers has crucial role in behavioural manifestation of attention problem delinquent behaviour, and aggression which are more less leads to social problem in later years of life. Furthermore it produced detrimental impact on behaviour in interaction with sex on total behaviour ($F=8.70$ $p<.01$) withdrawn (12.88 $p<.01$), somatic complaints ($F=9.52$ $P<.01$), anxiety (4.98 $p<.05$), Social problem ($F=12.47$ $p<.01$), thought problem (8.79 $P<.01$) attention problem ($F=16.13$ $P<.01$), aggression ($F=5.47$ $P<.05$), and other behaviour problems ($F=7.35$ $P<.01$). This indicate the importance of the psycho-socio-somatic health status of the mother with reference to growth and development of children. The results gave a deep insight in the area of behaviour modification, that can be achieved through counselling the mothers on their physical and mental health aspects. Further, it appeared that mothers suffering from any kind of psycho-social-somatic health problems will be unable to look after their children, qualitatively which in turn produces manifest behavioural problem in children.*

The subject, growth and development of children has received serious attention of academicians, policy makers and practitioners; scholars of social work and sociology who have placed the child at a focal point of their researches. These researchers have aimed at understanding scientifically and systematically the determinants and detrimental factors related to growth and development in the developmental processes of the child (Vidya, 1998; Vidya and Tripathi 1998; Tripathi and Vidya, 2000). The family environment plays a significant role in the behavioural pattern of the child. The cordial environment in the family which can only be possible in one condition when mother's health and social status in the family and society is considerably satisfactory, secondly, the health and well being of the given child who has to interact with the environment for accomplishment of modest behaviour (Vidya and Tripathi, 2001). The sensory equipment through which the experiences are derived at birth, are neither fully developed, nor adequate enough for initiating these experiences that are necessary to generate complex set of adjustive behaviour (Sears, 1975). Therefore, during the period of childhood any amount of deprivation either in the form of poor nutritional status and inadequate stimulation and care leads to manifestation of aberrated behaviour (Misra and Tripathi 1980; Tripathi, 1993; Tripathi, Rani and Vidya, 1998).

The recent studies on development provides no single ultimate truth instead, it offers a explanations about how the child grows, facing us to pick and choose, leaving us uncomfortable and unsure, about our current convictions, and motivating us to seek additional knowledge as the basis for our choices (Vidya, 1998; Scarr,1985). Great diversity characterizes the interests and concerns of the thousands of investigators, who study child development. But all the child developmental researchers have a single goal in common, the desire to describe and identify those factors that influence the behaviour enactment that occur in young people during the first fifteen years of life.

The recent ecological studies focused on impact of school setting, suggest that pupils attending small schools as compared to large high school received an qualitative extra curricular experience, needless to say the felt responsibility to become involved in such activities and real participation led to acquisition of leadership and responsibilities. The pupil of small schools did not participate well as a result the leadership related qualities found to be less among them (Barker and Gump 1964).

Taking the above into consideration it is clear that the child's behaviour greatly depends on the behavioural pattern of the other members in the family. But the relationship between the mother and the child being a primary factor, the mother's behaviour has a great impact on the child and its behaviour. This justifies the fact that mother's health status (Psychological, Social and Somatic) and her status in the family has to be good. If the Psycho, Socio, Somatic health status of the mother is poor, the mother will not be able to extend qualitative child care as a result the behaviour of the child deviates, leading to many other problems affecting the overall performance of the child so, the mother's Psycho, Socio, Somatic health status plays a vital role in child growth and development. The health status of the mother is influenced by many factors involved in the family environment. The family environment thus has to be congenial in order to have a healthy behavioural pattern among the members of the family (Tripathi and Vidya 1998). The family environment comprises, the ethnic community, geographical ecology, neighbourhood and the extent of the urbanization- The specific systems with which a family may interact are the political system, the economic system, media, education, health and legal system. When the family and its environment can't adapt to each other there exists a state of disequillibrium between the two. Family is vulnerable to disequilibrium not only because of change internally, but also because of inputs from external environment and caused behavioural disorders. (Tripathi 1992)

Since the external environment variables do not explain clearly the occurrence of behavioural disorders it becomes essential to analyse the environment of the children, needless to say it is the family more specifically the mother's health and behaviour characteristics. The child's growth and development strictly depends upon the degree of his/her competencies in meeting his/her bio-psychological needs within the family (Tripathi, Lakshmi Rani and Vidya 1998). The sensory organs which are required for deriving experiences from environment (family features eg. Family affective dynamics, quality of parenting, Psyco, Socio, Somatic health status of the mother) become sharpened and more efficacious in the development course of active interplay with environment in producing proper behaviour- Since the larger parts of the sensory inputs come from environment it can be easily assumed that growth and behaviour of a child should be shaped by the characteristics of environment in which the developing organism (child) is placed and to which it is exposed (Vidya, 1998), Hence the manifestation of behaviour disorders in childhood was studied in relation to the Psycho, Socio, Somatic health status of the mothers.

Method

Design

In the present piece of work an extensive survey was made to study the behavior disorders in children (5-12 years) in relation to the nature and magnitude of their maternal health status- (Psycho, Socio, Somatic problems of mothers) which followed a factorial type of research design.

The Psycho, Socio, Somatic health status is a property of individual subject therefore, exist naturally this has been measured with the help of Psycho, Socio, Somatic health status (PSSHS) questionnaire developed by the researcher (Vidya, 1997) for the present study. Hence the design employed in this study necessitated the use of the subject selection technique for manipulating the health aspects of mothers. Psycho, Socio, Somatic health status was the factor which provided basis for classification of subject in various comparison groups. Thus major experimental variable has to be considered as classification factor (Calfee, 1975). Apart from it the age and sex of children were also taken into account for developing an insight to the mechanism of deviant behaviour acquisition in childhood stage. Hence the present study employed *3x3x2* factorial design with 3 levels of Psycho, Socio, Somatic health status of the mother (mild/marked/severe) 3 age groups (60-84 months, 85-108 month, 109-144 months) and both the sex.

Sample

In the present study Psycho, Socio, Somatic health status questionnaires was administered to 600 mothers, having children (60 months - 144 months) in order to assess the nature and magnitude of Psycho, Socio, Somatic Health problems of mothers out of which only 360 mothers were selected using purposive sampling technique. The sample was well matched on age, sex, SES, nature and type of schools and general health status. There were 20 subjects in each cell with a total of 360 children and their parents. Thereafter the behavioural assessment of children was carried out in the school setup.

Tool

The present study confined to assess the behavioural disorders in children and its determinant in the family, more specifically the Psycho, Socio, Somatic health status of mother. Hence in the present piece of work two types of tools were used as mentioned below:

1. Psycho, Socio, Somatic, health status of mother (PSSHS) questionnaire.
2. Child behaviour check list.

PSSHS Questionnaire:

This was developed by the researcher to investigate the nature and magnitude of PSSHS among the mothers of the young children. It has three sub-components i.e.

a) Psychological health status
b) Social health status
c) Somatic health status

The above sub-components contain the items related to such kind of problems which are manifested in every day life situations, in order to investigate its determental influence on behaviour development at early childhood. This questionnaire also contains general demographic details about the parents, family composition, age, sex and about the child which was measured by 4 point scale.

Child behaviour check list: Developed by Achenbach (1983)

This check list provides a detailed profile of behaviour disorders manifested by children in terms of eight disorders. They are withdrawn behaviour, somatic complaints, anxious/ depressed, social disorder, thought disorder, attention disorder, delinquent behaviour and aggressive behaviour apart from it global over view of behaviour disorder, further more direction of behaviour disorders conclusive to personality abrasions with in the child and in social situations was obtained from 4 point scale behaviour check list.

Procedure

The first phase of the present study followed the procedure of an extensive survey of 600 mothers having children of age (60 months - 144 months) and both the sex as mentioned in the research design. The PSSHS questionnaire was administered to the mothers to investigate the nature and magnitude of Psycho, Socio, Somatic health status of mothers out of which 360 mothers and their children were considered using subject selection technique. Further in the second phase of the study children (60-144 months) were observed in the class-room situation on child behaviour checklist. The obtained data was qualitatively analysed (propotional analysis) and it was also treated to 3 way ANOVA.

In the present study an attempt has been made to analyse the prevalence of behaviour disorder in early childhood in response to age, sex and the level of psycho, socio, somatic health status of their mothers. Table 1 contains the frequency of different types of behavioural disorder. A close perusal of the table suggests that, majority of the children (72%) manifest behavioural disorders varying from mild (MLD) to severe (SV). However, the marked (MKD) behavioural disorder (29.16%) found to be prominent one followed by severe (20.27%), moderate (12.5%) to mild (MLD) (10:29%).

TABLE - 1

Level of Behavioural Disorder Manifested by Children (N = 360)

BEHAVIOURAL PROBLEM	LEVELS				
	Normal	Mild	Moderate	Marked	Severe
1. Overall	100 (27.74%)	37 (10.29%)	45 (12.5%)	105 (29.16%)	73 (20.27%)
2. Withdrawn	165 (45.83%)	95 (26.38%)	89 (24.72%)	8 (2.2%)	3 (<1%)
3. Somatic Complaint	118 (32.70%)	132 (36.66%)	63 (17.5%)	31 (8.61%)	16 (4.4%)
4. Anxiety	35 (9.72%)	152 (42.22%)	135 (37.5%)	29 (83.05%)	9 (3.5%)
5. Social Problem	92 (25.56%)	108 (30%)	89 (24.72%)	58 (16.11%)	13 (3.61%)
6. Thought Behaviour	115 (31.94%)	144 (40%)	71 (19.72%)	21 (5.83%)	9 (2.5%)
7. Attention Behaviour	250 (69.44%)	17 (4.72%)	34 (9.44%)	35 (9.72%)	24 (6.6%)
8. Del. Behaviour	139 (38.61%)	129 (35.83%)	70 (19.44%)	15 (4.16%)	7 (1.94%)
9. Agg. Behaviour	234 (65%)	22 (6.11%)	35 (9.72%)	58 (16.11%)	11 (3.05%)
10. Other Problem	161 (44.72%)	81 (22.5%)	65 (18.05%)	43 (11.94%)	10 (2.77%)
11. Externalising	223 (62.94%)	35 (10%)	35 (9.72%)	60 (16.66%)	6 (1.66%)
12. Internalising	225 (62.5%)	62 (17.5%)	37 (10.27%)	24 (6.66%)	12 (3.33%)

A critical examination of the table-1 revealed that, the incidence of various types behaviour disorders in children, were mild to severe. As far as severity of disorder is concerned attention disorder (6.6%) was prominent one followed by somatic complaints, social problem (3.61%) and aggression (3.05%). With reference to marked disordered social problem (16.11%) emerged as a major one followed by attention disorder (9.72%), somatic complaints (8-61%), anxiety (8-05%), thought disorder (5.83%). In case of moderate level of behaviour disorder majority of the children found to be manifesting more, anxiety (37.5%) followed withdrawn behaviour (24.72%), thought disorder (19.72%), delinquent behaviour (19.44%), somatic complaints (17.5%). As far as manifestation of behaviour disorder is concerned anxiety thought disorder and somatic complaints were found to be prominent in children, however its level vary from mild to severe. The trend of manifest behavioural disorder was also analysed. The result suggests that the emergence of thought disorder *and* somatic complaints manifested by children from mild to marked and severe. Whereas attention disorder either did not emerge or it is manifested marked to severe. The similar trend was found in case of anxiety behaviour.

TABLE - 2

Mean and Standard Deviation of Total Behavioural Disorder in Relation to Age and Sex (N=360)

AGE	MALE		FEMALE	
(in Months)	Mean	Standard Dev.	Mean	Standard Dev.
60 - 84	116.33	52.38	94.81	42.53
85 - 108	97.2	44.67	79.3	35.93
109 - 144	99.38	43.13	73.2	48.05

Table-2 contains the mean and standard deviation of total behavioural disorder in relation to age and sex of children. It is evident from the table that, male children manifest more behavioural disorders as compared their female counterparts. This might happen on account of socio-cultural perspective where different kinds of behaviour are expected from boy and girls which in turn lead to produce certain amount of complexes among children needless to say the variations are seen.

This occurs on two accounts, in first case, parents are more protective towards their male child with reference to feeding and physical comforts. Whereas in case of female child the parents are more overprotective with reference to her social interaction right from early childhood, which can be termed as gender discrimination.

Table 3 contains the mean and standard deviation of manifest behavioural disorder of children. It is evident from the table that aggression (mean = 14.93 ± 12.10), attention disorder (Mean = 12:76 ± 8.77) and anxiety (mean = 9.09 ± 4.84) found to be more prominent among other problems, a part from externalization (Mean = 15.45 ± 10.31) which was considerably more than internalization (Mean 12.43 ± 7.09).

TABLE - 3
Mean and Standard Deviation of Behavioural Disorder Manifested by Children (N = 360)

Behavioural Disorders	Mean	Standard Deviation
1. Overall	93.37	46.97
2. Withdrawn	3.4	2.99
3. Somatic Complaint	2.96	3.03
4. Anxiety	9.09	4.84
5. Social Problem	8.25	3.96
6. Thought Behaviour	2.63	2.04
7. Attention Behaviour	12.76	8.77
8. Del. Behaviour	5.62	3.18
9. Agg. Behaviour	14.93	12.18
10. Other Problem	5.83	4.22
11. Externalising	15.45	10.31
12. Internalising	12.43	7.09

An attempt has been made to analyse the impact of age, sex, and level of PSSHS of mother on manifestation of behavioural disorders, independently and in interaction with each other.

Table 4 contains the 3X3X2. 3 way ANOVA for total behavioural disorder. It is evident from the table that sex (F=20.78, df 13.42, P<.01) and age (F = 6.52, df 2,342, P< 01) emerged as a primary factor to produce significant influence on manifestation of behavioural disorder in children. Its quite surprising that level of PSSHS did not produce the main effect on manifestation of overall behavioural disorder. But, in interaction with age (F = 12.56, df 2.342 P<- 01) and sex (F = 8.70, df 2,342 P<.01) it has produced significant effect on manifestation of behavioural disorder in children.

TABLE - 4

Summary of 3x3x2 3 *way* ANOVA for Total Behaviour Disorder in Relation to Age of Children and PSSHS of Their Mothers and Sex (N = 360)

Source of Variation	df	Ms	F
A (AGE)	2	13502.602	6.52*
B (PSSH)	2	2885.811	1.39
C (SEX)	1	42989.87	20.78 **
A*B	2	25997.197	12.56 **
A*C	2	7388.0694	3.57*
B*C	2	18004-861	8.703 **
A* B*C	4	761302.91	368.02
ERROR	342	2068.5947	

** *P <. 01* * *P <. 05*

Discussion

After a very extensive and intensive investigation relating to behavioural abrasion's in early childhood, remedial measures for behaviour modification have to be spelt out. In order to evaluate the empirical findings of present work and making certain generalization, it seems appropriate to emphasize certain assumptions, which constitute the major planks of present work. Instead of taking traditional variables such as, socio-economic status, caste, class and culture as a major contributing factors to shape the personality makeup of children; in the present study the maternal characteristic (Rosenfeild 1992; Houston, Cates and Kelly 1992; Goodman, Adamson and Riniti and Cole 1994; Luerica, Hermosa 1985) has been considered as a major variable which may have direct (Farrel, 1980, Tripathi, 1992; Zinmerman 1989; Tripathi. Rani and Vidya, 1998) and/or indirect bearing on development of behaviour in children. Dadds (1986) found that for a group of multi problem families, the provision of intensive child management training was not sufficient to reduce generalised change in parent child interactions across family settings and times, the inclusion of procedure, aim specifically at enhancing generalization (planned activities for children, increasing marital and social support) was associated with generalised charge- Further families with marital discord, as well as the child behaviour problems, child management training produced immediate positive changes in parent child interaction but had little effect on the rates of aversive interchanges occurring between parents. A training procedure designed specifically for this, which (partner support training), produced decreases in these aversive interchanges and this effect was maintained at a six month follow up. Finally, a group comparison of the interaction between marital variables and treatment type revealed that while the inclusion of marital focused therapy aided the durability of parent and child treatment effects for marital discordant couples, little extra benefit was found for those with harmonious marriages. As extension of that review in present study, emphasis was given to the health status of mother in terms of psychological, social and somatic health along with variation in age and sex of children. There was a significant difference between male and female with regard to manifestation of behavioural disorder. This can be attributed to gender discrimination related attitude in Indian culture. In Indian society the expectation of parents vary in accordance with gender of their children (Tripathi, Rani and Vidya - 1988, Tripathi - 1992, Tripathi and Vidya - 1998). This trend indicates the detrimental and if mother is having some kind of problem, she always reflects on the girl child as compared to male child.

The finding of the present study indicate the role of PSSHS and sex related discriminations practiced in Indian society. As a matter of fact Indian women never manifest their emotional and social problems, as a result they fail to give quality care to their children which results in manifest behavioural disorders (Ainsworth, 1982; Rosenfield 1992) as a main effect of gender was found highly significant ($F = 20.78$;df 2.342 $P<.01$) followed by interaction effect of age of the children and Psycho, Socio, somatic health status of the mother ($F = 12.56$; df 2.342, $P<.01$). In the Indian Society, mothers having mild to marked health problems fail to give much attention, to their children, in this process they do not give required qualitative care and as a consequent reaction to it behaviour disorders emerged among the children.

Acquisition of Behaviour Disorder: A Dynamic Model

The obtained results in the present study clearly indicates that School going children acquire mild to moderate, behavioural disorder as a consequent reaction to environmental constraints and child care related inadequacies, needless to say which is the resultant of the level of PSSHS of mothers, Furthermore, it is evident from the study that, initially children acquire a mild deviation in behavioural manifestation, but on account of environmental negligence these deviations converts into behavioural disorder- Two types of theoretical explanation available for the emergence of manifest behavioural disorder in children. The first set of studies emphasize the role of negative environmental stimulation whereas the second set of studies emphasize the involvement of biological and genetic factors. It has been discussed that, child's home environment and his/her individual competences in meeting his/her biological and psycho, social needs with in the frame work of environmental facilities and constraints. Hence, it becomes necessary to consider the micro level factors e.g. the level of PSSHS of mothers in relation to manifestation of behavioural disorder. Fig – 1 present a model to explain the emergence of behavioural disorder among children.

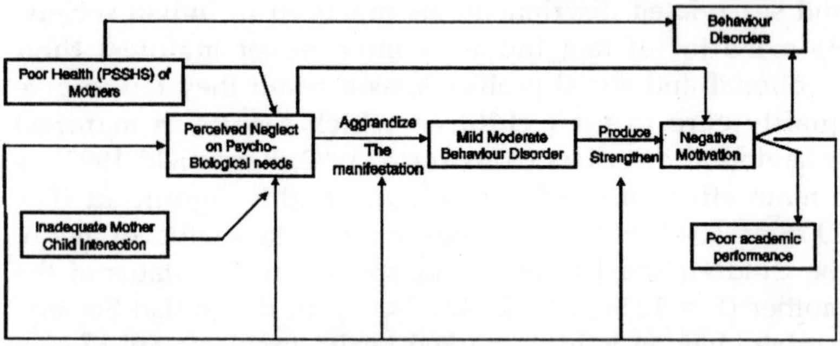

Fig. 1

ACQUISITION OF BEHAVIOUR DISORDER IN CHILDREN: A DYNAMIC MODEL

As far as the evidence of behavioural disorder in children is concerned it can be concluded that children tends to be less misbehaved if they come from a family where in quality childcare practices arc present- In other words it is commonly observed, that manifestation of aggressive and hostile behaviour is a result of aggressive environment at home number of studies emphasize the role of family environment and quality of mother child interaction which needles to say is determined by Psycho, Socio, Somatic health status of mother. Further there are studies which conclude that the personality make of the child makes him to behave aggressively in a given situation. This can be attributed to the motivational construct of the individual child. It has already been discussed the influence of child's home and inadequate mother child interaction on various aspect of human behaviour. Hence the contention of present study is the question of manifest behaviour disorder and poor academic performance has to he considered by taking the home environment and PSSHS level of mothers into consideration. Fig - 1 explains the acquisition process of behaviour disorder in early childhood.

The model postulates that inadequate home environment for a child, operating due to poor PSSHS of mother is likely to influence the motivational construct of the child negatively. This negative motivation will not allow the child to perform well on scholastic achievements as well as a modest behaviour at home and school situations. Poor performance at school may reinforce the aggression level of mother at home. In other words what may start out as mildly unsupportive interms of neglect on Psycho, biological needs tend to become more and more with advancement in child's age.

The differences in the model presented above and other models of behaviour acquisition in childhood stage lies in emphasizing the primary of motivational variables and the role they play in the acquisition of certain behaviour, as a resultant of maltreatments given by their mothers on account of their poor PSSH status. As a matter of fact children differ in their behaviour enactments in a given situation to begin with manifestation of aggression (Tripathi, Rani, Vidya, 1998, Vidya 1998) as consequent reaction to poor family environment (Vidya and Tripathi, 2001). A study by (Tripathi, Rani and Vidya, 2001) provides ample proof that these differences wider with advancing age and vowing to variations in ordinal position as a consequent reaction to environmental stress (Tripathi and Vidya, 1999).

The model also postulates that perceived neglect on Psycho biological needs aggravated the manifestation of mild to moderate behaviour disorder and negative motivation. This may happen in two ways, firstly it is possible that because of poor academic performance children do not feel enthusiastic enough to interact positively in a given social situation which further hampers the quality interaction between mother and child more specifically if mother is suffering from PSSHS disorders.

REFERENCES

Achenbach. T.M& Eddbrock. C.S (1983). Manual for the child behaviour check list and revised child behaviour profile Buligton, V.T. Queen City Printer.

Ainsworth. M.D (1982). Attachment Retrospect and Prospect. In C.M barkes and J. Stevenson Hindle (Eds). The place of attachment in human behaviour New York; Basic Book,

Andrews. S.R, Blumenthal. J.B, Jonnson. D.L, Kahn, AJ. Ferguson. C.J, Laster. T.M, Malone. P.E and Wallece. D.B (1982). The skills of mothering - a study of parent - child development centers. Monograph of the Society for Research in Child Development 47 (6, serial No.198).

Barker R.G., and Gump, P,V(1964). Big School, Small school: High School size and student behaviour, Stanford, CA: Stanford University Press.

Calfee. R,C. (1975). Human Experimental Psychology. N.Y: Holt.

Dadds.M.R (1986). The role of marital variables in the treatment of conduct disorders of childhood, doctorate thesis (041), University Kansas.

Farrel. J.A. (1980). Parental and child, change in Adlterian study groups Monographic, University of Sas Kutchewan, Faculty of Education staff study.

Goodman S.H, Adamson L.B, Riniti J, Cole. S, (1994). Mother's expressed, attitudes associations with maternal depression and children's self-esteem and psychopathology, *Journal of Academic, Child, Adolescent, Psychiatry. Nov-Dec* pp. 0890-8567.

Houston.B-K., Cates OS; Kelly K.E. (1992). Job Stress, Psychological Strain and health problems in women employed full time out of the home and home makers, *Journal article*-Department of Psychology, University of Kansas, Lawrence. pp.66045-2160.

Luerica M., Hermosa B (1995), Maternal reports of behaviour problems reports of behaviour problems in pre school hispanic children: on exploratory study in preventive paediatrics, *Journal of National Medicine Association,. Department of Psychology, Montclair State University, Montclair New Jersey, USA. December,*

Pp.0027-9684.

Misra.G. and Tripathi.L.B (1980). Psychological consequences of prolonged deprivation. Agra National Psychological Corporation-

Rosenfleld.JA (1992). Maternal work outside the home and its effect of Women and their families, *Journal of American Medicine Women Association.* Department of family medicine, East Tennessee of State University in Bristol. *March, April issue. 00913-B421.*

Scarr.S. (1985). Constructing Psychology: Making facts and fables for our times. *American Psychologist, 40,* Pp. 499-512.

Sears, R.R. (1976). Ycur ancients revisited: A history of child development. In E.M. Hetherington (Ed.), Review of child development research (Vol-5, pp.1-73) Chicago University of Chicago Press.

Tripathi.S.K. (1992). Socio-Cultural correlates of malnutrition in early childhood and its behavioural consequences, unpublished paper, National institute of public co-operation and Child development, SRC, Bangalore.

Tripathi.S.K. and Lakshmi Ran. D (1993), Aggression acquision in Childhood, A critical review unpublished paper. N1PCCD. SRC-Bangalore.

Tripathi.S.K., Lakshmi Rani.D. and Vidya.C (1999). Social Class and Aggression acquisition in childhood *Journal of Psychological Researches 42(3)/98.*

Tripathi.S.K and Vidya-C (1999) Crowding and Human Behaviour in next millenium: Some issues. *Journal of Psychological Research Vol. 43(2)* Pp. *39-45.*

Tripathi. S.K., and Vidya. C (2003). Child development: A psycho – biological perspective, Journal of psychological research Vol-47(2).P.33-40.

Vidya.C, Padma.K, Tripathi.S.K. (1997) Behavioural Consequences of malnutrition Some issues, Paper Published in Proceedings of nutrition Society of India, Hyderabad, P.44.

Vidya.C. (1998). Psycho. Socio, Somatic Correlates of mother and behaviour problem in Children department of Home Science,

Unpublished desertaion, Bangalore.

Vidya. C. and Tripathi. S.K. (1998) Behaviour problems in childhood is correlated and consequences a paper presented in international APSSAM Conference, Yogyakarta, Indonesia, December 7-11,131.

Vidya. C *and*. Tripathi. S-K (2001). Family and mental health: perspectives of prevention and management in 21st Century, *Social Science internatuional, Intel disciplinary readings, ISSN. 0970-1087 Vol.17 (1) pp. 25 – 35.*

Zinmerman. S.L. (1989). Understanding family policy. Theoretical approaches, London Sage Publications.

12

Changing Social Realties in Teaching Profession and Job Burnout

Its Correlates and Consequences

Vinay C. and Tripathi S. K.

Job burnout is a malaise of the spirit in which motivation, that mysterious force that gets us moving is damaged or even destroyed. Job burnout could be called job depression. Job burnout is not an all-or-nothing proposition. On any particular day enthusiasm for work is increasing or decreasing but it does not remain the same. Even the hottest fire will burn out, so we tend them fanning, stoking, and occasionally adding another log. When motivation wanes, we burn out. Occasional feelings of frustration, anger, depression, dissatisfaction, and anxiety are normal parts of living and working. But people caught in the Job burnout cycle usually experience these negative emotions more often until they become chronic. In the worst cases, people complain of a kind of emotional fatigue or depletion. While no two people respond in exactly the same way, people tend to experience frustration first that may evolve into anger. In later stages we see anxiety and fear, then depression and, in extreme cases, despair. These physical symptoms are accompanied by declining performance, withdrawal and interpersonal problems, substance abuse in an attempt to self-medicate, illness, absenteeism, and feelings of meaninglessness. Hence Job burnout is not stress, although constant stress is one of the causes and earlier stages of developing Job burnout. Interestingly, Job burnout often starts with a life change that comes with high expectations for happiness and/or success Job burnout resulted from a variety of factors. The present study was formulated to investigate the nature and magnitude of job burnout among the school teachers, the differentials in job burnout due to variations in age, sex, job satisfaction, self-perception; a well matched sample on socio-demographic variables such as age, sex, professional experience and total family income was taken to draw a general conclusion. Among the variable attribution of professional success found to be highly correlated with the level of job-burnout followed by professional experience, age and self- perception and locus of control that is internal. Job satisfaction level increases with advancing age. The self perception interim of teaching found to be influenced by family income followed by age. Attribution of professional success can be predicated by professional experience and family income, further it is influenced by external forces operating in school environment then that of internal locus of control.

The historical prospective of educational practices in organized and formal child education have received a great importance in recent years. In India education of children has a long past-start from gurukul system to day school system. The quality of education influenced by the motivational construct personality make up of the teachers. In psychological theorization motivation is posited to explain the dynamic properties of human behavior such as persistence, perseverance, vigor, commitment, in order to accomplish the organizational goal i.e. effective teaching.

The differentials in teaching techniques have led to conuceptualisation of "need" which has been conceived basically as a deficiency of something vital to style of teaching. In other words the level of job satisfaction perceived, self-perception, attribution of professional success, needless to say, explains the level of job burnout among the teachers. In teaching profession few things is essential to make teaching effective such as-

1) skill variety
2) task identity

3) task significance
4) autonomy
5) feed back

The term skill variety refers to the degree to which the job requires a variety of different activities so the teachers can use a number of skills and talent in order to make their teaching effective. This is required on account of repetition of similar copies and content year of year. Secondly, the task identify refers to completion to whole or identifiable (syllabus, portion). Piece of work and; task significance refers to the substantial impact of teaching on the achievement of pupil studying under kind supervision of the teacher. The autonomy increases substantial freedom, independence and description to the teachers in scheduling their work and determining the methods and techniques to be used in teaching.

In the present context, by virtue of, stress for completion of syllabus within limited period of time, apart from organizing periodical tests, examination carrying out extra curricular activities, teachers are unable to achieve the above mentioned phenomenon make their teaching qualitative in classroom situation.

The success of any school system depends on how well it is brought in function or fabricated and how well it is effective. Thus, human resource not only constitute the most vital input but also the most strategic and critical determinants for the growth and development of school environment while material efficiency and technical skills have made rapid strides, to commensurate progress in the knowledge and dynamics of human behavior at work is less evinced. The problems like absenteeism low morale and dissatisfaction at various levels plague the management, which if neglected might weaken the very structure of school system. The search for exploring teaching the teaching behavior of teachers has yielded both interesting and useful data. The concern, for the humanness for the teacher is strongly reflected in pioneering work of several educationalist, human development expert, psychologist, is of recent origin. The environment or work setting within which modern teacher lives can be termed as social technical system, that explain the level of attaining satisfactory experience of the teacher.

Job Burnout: A Conceptual Analysis

Burnout is a malaise of the spirit in which motivation, that mysterious force that gets us moving is damaged or even destroyed, job burnout could be called job depression. Burnout is not an all-or-nothing proposition. On any particular day enthusiasm for work is increasing or decreasing but it does not remain the same. Even the hottest fire will burn out, so we tend them fanning, stoking, and occasionally adding another log. When motivation wanes, we burn out.

In other words, occasional feelings of frustration, anger, depression, dissatisfaction, and anxiety are normal parts of living and working. But people caught in the burnout cycle usually experience these negative emotions more often until they become chronic. In the worst cases, people complain of a kind of emotional fatigue or depletion. While no two people respond in exactly the same way, people tend to experience frustration first that may evolve into anger. In later stages we see anxiety and fear then depression and in extreme cases, despair. These physical symptoms are accompanied by declining performance, withdrawal and interpersonal problems, substance abuse in an attempt to self-medicate, illness and absenteeism. Job burnout is a response to work stress that leaves of feeling powerless, hopeless, fatigued, drained and frustrated. But since job burnout is not an overnight occurrence, it's important to recognize its early signs and to act before the problem becomes truly serious.

Job Burn-Out: Reconceptualisation as Perspectives of Teaching Profession

The term job burnout refers to the physiological state of mind that makes the person feel exhausted and develop bordem out of his/her work at work place. Numerous study indicated that job burnout get manifested on account of ambiguous job structure and its characteristics and lack of ambiguous job structure and its characteristics; and lack of job satisfaction (Locke, 1969; Caldwell, 1957; Dewar and Verval, 1979; Anderson, 1985). In other words job burn-out is conceived as negative emotional state resulting from the appraisal once job or job experience, implies that individual will lose energy in maintaining or increasing pleasurable experience and minimizing or decreasing unpleasant experience.

Gaylord's (1992) found no differences in race or gender, but younger workers did tend to be more burned out than older people. Gaylord also found that the effectiveness of coping skills depended on the person's personality. Working much harder or much less helped emotionally unstable or negative-thinking in people. They seemed to feel less emotionally exhausted by taking it easy at work, or by working extremely hard, which may make them feel better about their productivity. However, a change in work effort hurt people who tend to think positively. People with a lot of self-worth learned a long time ago what the right amount of work for them is. They just keep chugging along.

The positive and negative thinkers responded differently when coping by seeking social support. An emotionally stable person will feel better when talking with other people about work, yet will also do quite well by not talking about work. People who feel good about themselves don't need others to validate that, they can work problems out for themselves. But emotionally unstable people are better off if they do not increase or decrease the amount of social support they receive. Not talking about their problems will make their burnout worse, because they have to get their troubles off of their chests. But talking too much will also hurt them." If a person with high neurotic tendencies talks a lot to other people about their troubles at work, I think it makes them ruminate about it too much.

Downey, Hemenover and Rappoport (2001) developed a three- to four-week training programme that combined Internet information, group sessions and diaries written by the study subjects. Their most recent study used 101 employed college students. Some students were given training specific to their emotional tendencies. People who showed a tendency toward negative thinking in tests were given different training than emotionally stable workers. But the study found little burnout among student employees, so the coping strategies were of little use. They are planning another study, which will use the coping strategies on full-time employees. Signs of burnout include emotional exhaustion, withdrawal from other people at work, and unhappiness about accomplishments at work. Not surprisingly, negative people are more likely to feel these symptoms.

Job burnout is typically seen as a reaction to the work that people have a high burnout rate if there is a lot of role ambiguity or role conflict, or if they are working in places with a lot of potentially negative contact with people.

Causes of Job Burnout

Burnout is not stress, although constant stress is one of the causes and earlier stages of developing burnout. Interestingly, burnout often starts with a life change that comes with high expectations for happiness and/or success, such as a new job. If the job changes, underutilizes the employee's skills, or is not what the employee expected - or if she never receives positive or useful feedback - stress may result. Short-term stress, like the kind that comes with working on a project, can be exhilarating and rewarding, helping you to get your job done. It's when the stress is chronic and unrelenting that burnout is most likely to set in. The burnout results from a variety of factors.

Methodology

Design

The present study was formulated to investigate the nature and magnitude of job-burnout, prominent among teachers, teaching in preprimary, primary and higher secondary standards in and around Bangalore city. Job burnout is an individual characteristic feature and, therefore, exists naturally but as a consequent reaction to several occupational, social and personal attributes. Needless to say it requires a systematic study. In order to draw a general conclusion sample was matched on socio-demographic variables such as age, sex, professional experience and total family income. In the present study precision has been taken while selecting the sample to accomplish objectives.

Sample

In accordance with the research design the sample was drawn from Institutions at Bangalore. There were eight preprimary school teachers, twenty five primary school teachers and eleven teachers teaching in Higher Secondary and Secondary level with the total of 44.

Tool

In order to have comprehensive information about job burnout and its various personal and social determinants following measures (Self rating Schedule) were used i.e., Job satisfaction scale; self perception schedule; Job burn out scale.

Procedure

The above tools were administered to the teachers with their prior consent for participating in the present study. The tools were administered to teachers in a fixed time. The required clarifications were made in answering the questions and very few teachers took more than two hours for filling the questionnaire.

Results

Job Satisfaction

Table 1 contains level of job satisfaction in relation to age of the subject. It is evident from the table that majority of the teachers had high (17) level of job satisfaction followed by average (16) and (11) teachers has low level of job satisfaction. The striking point that has emerged from the table is increase in the level of job satisfaction corresponding with advancing in age that can be attributed to contentment with the nature of job.

TABLE - 1

Level of Job Satisfaction in Relation to Age

Age in years	Level of Job Satisfaction in Relation to Age			
	Low	*Average*	*High*	*Total*
25-30	2	3	4	9
31-35	4	1	2	7
36-40	3	3	4	10
40 and above	2	9	7	18
Total	11	16	17	44

Table 2 indicated similar pattern in relation to professional experience with a slight variation. Majority of less experience teachers had low to average level of job satisfaction, contrary to that highly experienced teachers had high level of job satisfaction. Job satisfaction is directly related with professional experience. In relation to income, mixed pattern (table 3) was found with regard to level of job satisfaction.

TABLE - 2

Level of Job Satisfaction in Relation to Professional Experience

Experience in years	Level of Job Satisfaction in Relation to Professional Experience			
	Low	*Average*	*High*	*Total*
Up to 5 years	6	6	5	17
6-11	3	2	3	8
12 and above	2	8	9	19
Total	11	16	17	44

TABLE - 3
Level of Job Satisfaction in Relation to Family Income

Family Income	Level of Job Satisfaction in Relation to Family Income			
	Low	*Average*	*High*	*Total*
High	2	4	5	11
Medium	5	7	5	17
Low	4	5	7	16
Total	11	16	17	44

Self Perception

Another measure was used in order to assess the level of self perception in terms of teaching method acceptance among the students self perception it was found that majority of the teacher manifested average trend followed by high and low self perception (Table 4).

TABLE - 4
Level of Self Perception in Relation to Age

Age in years	Level of Self Perception in Relation to age			
	Low	*Average*	*High*	*Total*
25-30	2	6	1	9
31-35	0	4	3	7
36-40	2	5	3	10
40 and above	6	5	7	18
Total	10	20	14	44

The Table 4 suggests that level of self perception found average by and large.

In case of young and middle age teachers. Whereas teachers above 40 yrs manifested steeper increase in self perception corresponding to their age.

As far as level of self perception in relation to professional experienced is concerned, majority of the teachers manifested low to average self perception (table 5) but less and highly experienced teacher had high level of self perception.

TABLE - 5

Level of Self Perception in Relation to Professional Experience

Experience in years	Level of Self Perception in relation to Professional experience			
	Low	*Average*	*High*	*Total*
Up to 5 years	3	8	6	17
6-11 years	1	5	2	8
12 years and above	6	7	6	19
Total	10	20	14	44

Role of family income (Table 6) on self perception had all together different trend. Teachers with low and medium income had low to average self perception in majority whereas teachers with high income had high self perception and low to average self perception equally.

TABLE - 6

Level of Self Perception in Relation to Family Income

Family Income in Rs	Level of Self Perception in Relation to Family income			
	Low	*Average*	*High*	*Total*
High	3	2	6	11
Medium	5	9	3	17
Low	5	9	5	19
Total	10	20	14	44

Vinay. C (2002), A study on Job Burnout Among school teachers in an educational and institution, unpublished project report, submitted to Bangalore University.

Mottaz, C.J. (1987), Age and work satisfaction work and occupation, 14(3), 387-409.

Sharan, R (1980). Working condition and Job satisfaction among industrial women workers. Indian Journal of Industrial Relations 18: 121-131

Weber M (1947) Theory of Social and economic organization. Organizational Behavior and Human performance, 16:74-113.

White, T.A. and Spector E.P.(1978). An Investigation of Age related factors in the age- job satisfaction relationship. Psychology and aging, 2(3), 261-165.